Building SPELLING Skills

Grade 3

Daily Practice

Spelling Strategies

Say a word correctly.

- Don't leave out or mispronounce sounds.
- Write the sounds in the correct order.

Think about what the word looks like.

- Think about how the spelling pattern looks.
- Write it, look at it, and decide if it looks correct.

Look for small words in spelling words.

- spin—**pin, in**
- cupcake—**cup, cake**

Look at syllables in spelling words.

- Spell the word one syllable at a time.
  remember—**re • mem • ber**

Use rhyming words to help spell a word.

- If you can spell **book**, you can spell **look**.

Use rules for adding endings.

- Drop silent **e** before adding a suffix.
- Double the final consonant before adding a suffix.
- Change the final **y** to **i** and add **es**.

How to Study Your List

1 Read and Spell

2 Copy and Spell

3 Cover and Spell

4 Uncover and Check

Building **Spelling** Skills

WEEK 1

Spelling List

This Week's Focus:

- Spell short and long **a** words
- Spell words with the endings **-ed** and **-ing**
- Add the endings **-ed** and **-ing** after dropping the silent **e**
- Recognize the short **e** sound in **said**

STEP 1 Read and Spell	STEP 2 Copy and Spell	STEP 3 Cover and Spell
1. said	______	______
2. ask	______	______
3. stand	______	______
4. catch	______	______
5. eight	______	______
6. afraid	______	______
7. away	______	______
8. always	______	______
9. playing	______	______
10. waved	______	______
11. takes	______	______
12. than	______	______
13. great	______	______
14. they	______	______
15. prey	______	______
16. ______ bonus word	______	______
17. ______ bonus word	______	______

fold

Visual Memory

Fill in the boxes.

stand	waved	great	than	prey
afraid	they	playing	ask	takes
away	said	eight	catch	always

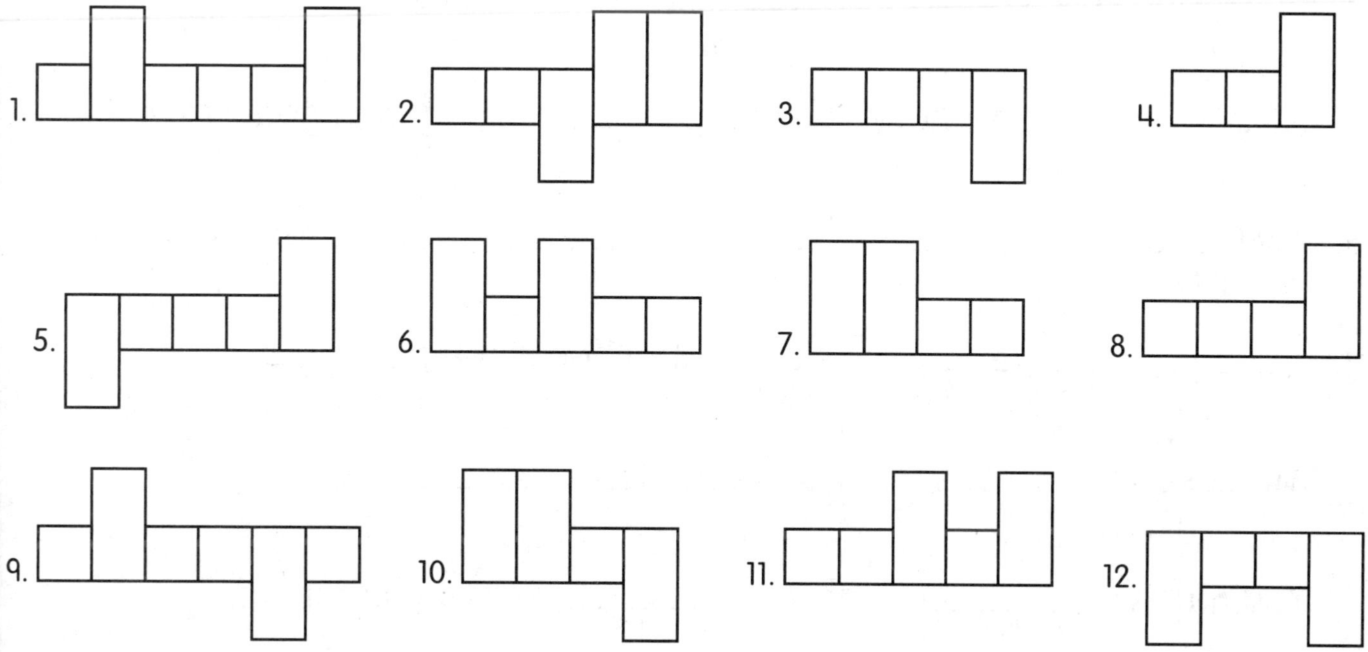

Cross out the misspelled words.

1. ~~sed~~	said	8. they	thay
2. eitgh	eight	9. aks	ask
3. great	grait	10. stend	stand
4. prey	drey	11. playing	paling
5. catsh	catch	12. taks	takes
6. afraid	ufraid	13. than	fhan
7. wavd	waved	14. away	uway

Word Meaning

Fill in the missing words.

takes	ask	always	catch	eight
afraid	away	stand	prey	waved
said	than	great	they	playing

1. An octopus uses its __________ arms to catch its __________.
2. It __________ a long time to __________ my dog to give him a bath.
3. My little sister is __________ __________ of thunder and lightning.
4. __________ were __________ football at the park.
5. Marcus __________ his hand and __________, "Good-bye."
6. You must __________ far __________ from the campfire.

My Spelling Dictation

Write the sentences. Circle the spelling words.

1. ____________________

____

____

2. ____________________

____

____

Word Study

Underline the words with the long **a** sound.
Circle the letters that make that sound.

waved	catch	away	takes	great
ask	eight	stand	said	they
always	afraid	prey	than	playing

An ending is a word part added at the end of a word.
Add **ed** and **ing** to each word.

	ed	ing
1. play	played	playing
2. ask		
3. prey		
4. paint		

Drop the **e** and add the endings **ed** and **ing**.

1. wave	waved	waving
2. smile		
3. skate		
4. bake		

Building Spelling Skills WEEK 2

Spelling List

This Week's Focus:

- Spell short **e** words
- Spell words with the long **e** sound spelled **ea**, **ie**, **ee**, **e**, and **y**
- Recognize the short **i** sound in **been**

STEP 1 Read and Spell	STEP 2 Copy and Spell	STEP 3 Cover and Spell
1. next		
2. left		
3. help		
4. please		
5. believe		
6. many		
7. very		
8. been		
9. seen		
10. she		
11. between		
12. three		
13. easy		
14. sea		
15. leave		
16. ______ bonus word		
17. ______ bonus word		

fold

Visual Memory

Fill in the boxes.

very	believe	next	easy	leave
been	please	help	between	she
seen	many	left	three	sea

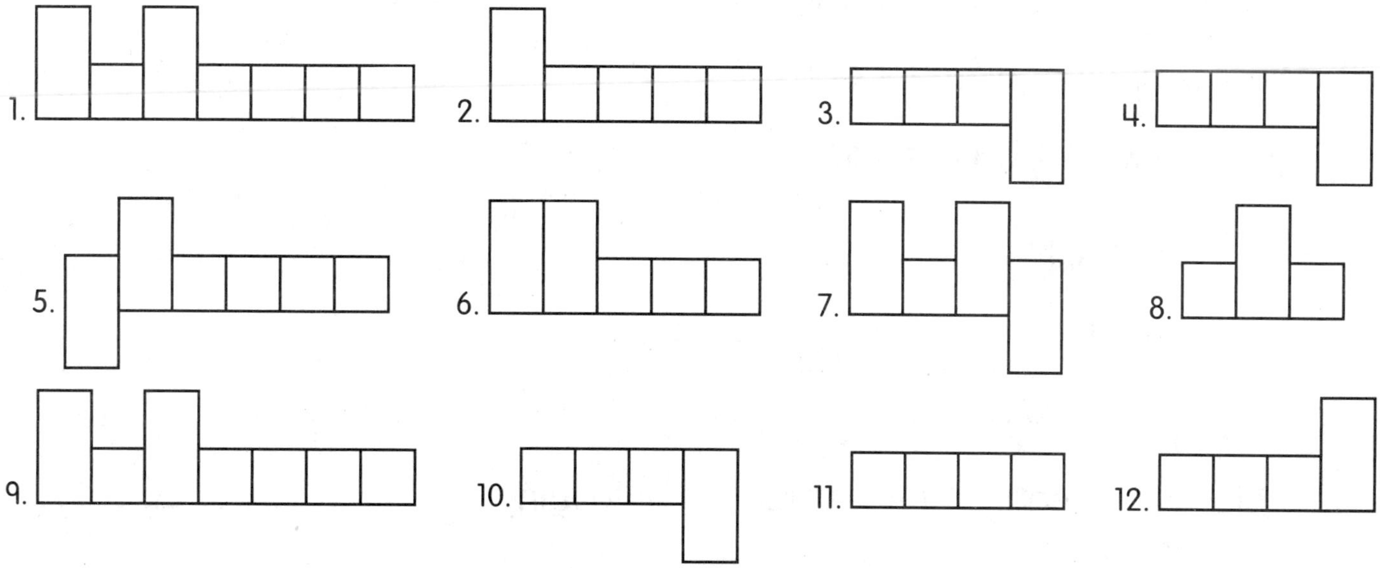

Circle the misspelled words. Write them correctly on the lines.

1. Plez help me fix my bike. ________________
2. We have to leaf now. ________________
3. It isn't eezy to ride a horse. ________________
4. Have you ben to the park? ________________
5. Park the car betwene the trees. ________________
6. Did you belive his story? ________________
7. I saw miny cows at his farm. ________________
8. Jane had tree pet cats. ________________

Word Meaning

Answer the questions.

next	left	help	please	believe
many	very	been	seen	she
between	three	easy	sea	leave

1. What comes after **two**? ____________
2. What is another word for **ocean**? ____________
3. What is the opposite of... ?

   difficult ____________ stay ____________

   right ____________ harm ____________

   few ____________
4. Which word means "in the middle of two things"? ____________
5. What word do you use if you want to show good manners? ____________
6. Which word means you think something is true? ____________

My Spelling Dictation

Write the sentences. Circle the spelling words.

1. ____

____

____

2. ____

____

____

Word Study

Underline the words with the long **e** sound.
Circle the letters that make that sound.

three	left	she
please	believe	many
very	been	seen
help	between	leave
easy	sea	next

Write the spelling words that rhyme with these words.

1. merry	__________	6. pea	__________
2. any	__________	7. queen	__________
3. sneeze	__________	8. relieve	__________
4. free	__________	9. bee	__________
5. yelp	__________	10. lean	__________

next	left	help	please	believe
many	very	been	seen	she
leave	three	easy	sea	between

Building Spelling Skills WEEK 3

Spelling List

This Week's Focus:

- Spell short and long **i** words
- Spell words in the **-ind**, **-ile**, **-ight**, and **-ink** word families

STEP 1 Read and Spell

STEP 2 Copy and Spell

STEP 3 Cover and Spell

fold

1. pitch ______ ______
2. drink ______ ______
3. swim ______ ______
4. life ______ ______
5. while ______ ______
6. I ______ ______
7. my ______ ______
8. light ______ ______
9. buy ______ ______
10. eye ______ ______
11. which ______ ______
12. find ______ ______
13. why ______ ______
14. kind ______ ______
15. try ______ ______
16. ______ (bonus word) ______ ______
17. ______ (bonus word) ______ ______

Visual Memory

Fill in the boxes.

life	pitch	my	eye	why
drink	while	light	which	kind
try	I	buy	find	swim

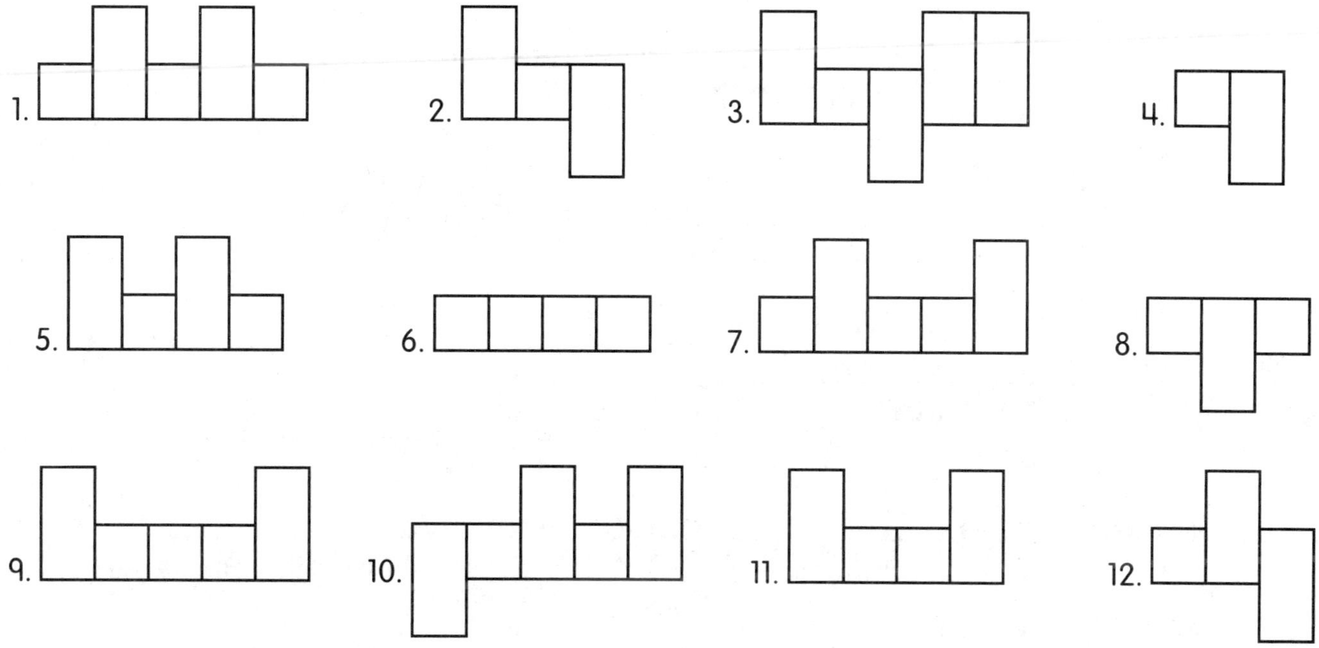

Circle the misspelled words.
Write them correctly on the lines.

1. Mom needs to bie a lite for the lamp. ________ ________
2. Witch kind of drenk do you like best? ________ ________
3. Trie to catch the ball when I picth it. ________ ________
4. I get water in my aye when I swem. ________ ________
5. Eye like to by that kind of pen. ________ ________

Word Meaning

Fill in the missing words.

1. ____________ (I, try) have something in my ____________ (why, eye).

2. ____________ (Why, Try) did you ____________ (buy, which) that kind of soft ____________ (drink, pitch)?

3. ____________ (Which, Witch) kind of ____________ (while, light) do you need?

4. Can you catch ____________ (while, light) I ____________ (why, pitch) the baseball?

5. The words ____________ (my, find) and ____________ (try, while) rhyme.

6. I have tried to be a ____________ (find, kind) person all of my ____________ (while, life).

My Spelling Dictation

Write the sentences. Circle the spelling words.

1. ____

____

____

2. ____

____

____

Word Study

Underline the words with the long **i** sound.
Circle the letters that make that sound.

life	drink	try
pitch	while	I
my	light	buy
eye	which	find
why	kind	swim

Add letters to make new words.
Then read all the words in each word family.

ind	ile	ight	ink
f ind	____ile	____ight	____ink
____ind	____ile	____ight	____ink
____ind	____ile	____ight	____ink
____ind	____ile	____ight	____ink

Building Spelling Skills WEEK 4

Spelling List

This Week's Focus:

- Spell words with the long **o** sound
- Distinguish between one- and two-syllable words

STEP 1 Read and Spell	STEP 2 Copy and Spell	STEP 3 Cover and Spell
1. rocket		
2. pocket		
3. hold		
4. told		
5. often		
6. grow		
7. throne		
8. so		
9. sew		
10. most		
11. almost		
12. both		
13. coach		
14. open		
15. also		
16. ______ bonus word		
17. ______ bonus word		

fold

Visual Memory

Fill in the boxes.

rocket	hold	often	grow	so
pocket	told	also	sew	most
throne	almost	both	coach	open

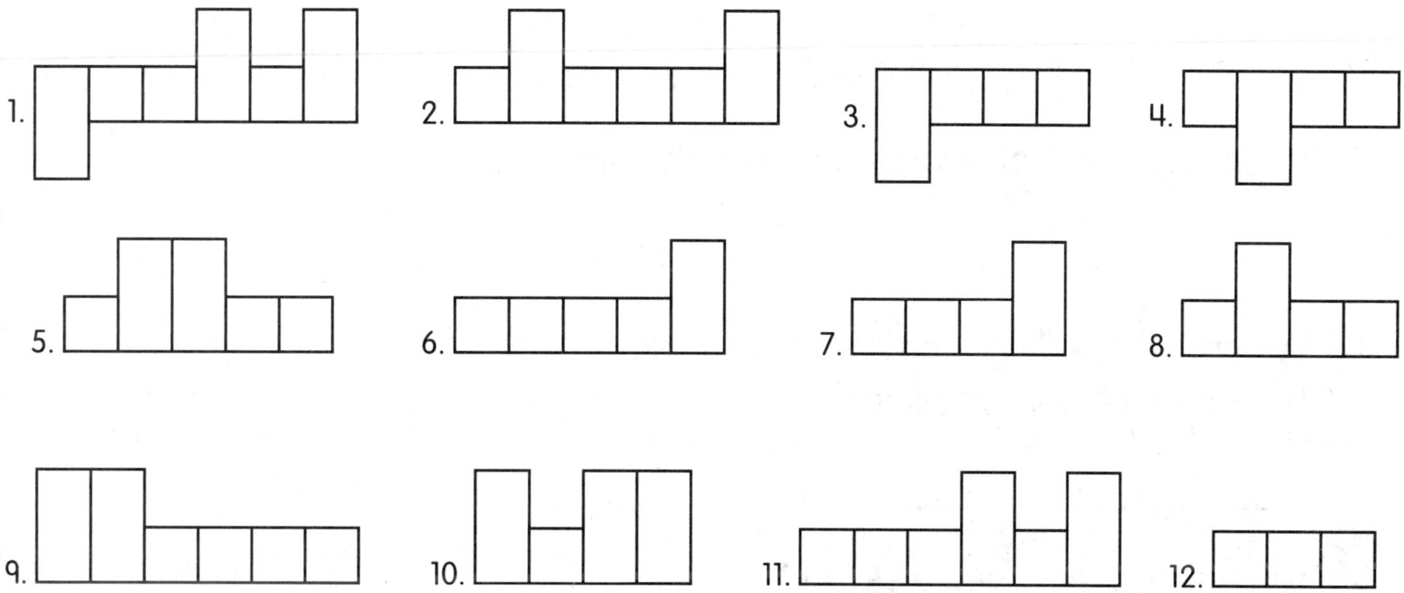

Cross out the misspelled words.

1. roket	rocket	7. coach	koach
2. whold	hold	8. allso	also
3. often	offen	9. opun	open
4. throne	thone	10. grow	groe
5. amolst	almost	11. told	tole
6. both	bofh	12. sowe	sew

Word Meaning

Answer the questions.

rocket	hold	often	grow	so
pocket	most	also	sew	told
throne	almost	both	coach	open

1. What could a king or queen sit on? ____________
2. In what part of a jacket can you carry things? ____________
3. Which two spelling words rhyme with **cold**?

   ____________ ____________

4. Which two spelling words sound the same but have different spellings?

   ____________ ____________

5. What is the opposite of **shut**? ____________
6. What transportation would an astronaut use? ____________

My Spelling Dictation

Write the sentences. Circle the spelling words.

1. ____________________

   ____

   ____

2. ____________________

   ____

   ____

Word Study

Underline the words with the long **o** sound.
Circle the letters that make that sound.

grow	hold	throne
rocket	so	pocket
told	also	sew
most	often	almost
both	coach	open

Say each word.

rocket	hold	often	both	almost
grow	so	pocket	coach	throne
told	also	sew	open	most

Write the words with one syllable.

1. ____________
2. ____________
3. ____________
4. ____________
5. ____________
6. ____________
7. ____________
8. ____________
9. ____________

Write the words with two syllables.

1. ____________
2. ____________
3. ____________
4. ____________
5. ____________
6. ____________

Building Spelling Skills WEEK 5

Spelling List

This Week's Focus:

- Spell words with the short and long **u** sounds
- Spell words with an initial /**y**/ sound

STEP 1 Read and Spell | STEP 2 Copy and Spell | STEP 3 Cover and Spell

fold

1. under
2. such
3. much
4. young
5. touch
6. use
7. your
8. you
9. unit
10. cute
11. few
12. new
13. fuel
14. human
15. music
16. ______ bonus word
17. ______ bonus word

Visual Memory

Unscramble the letters to make spelling words.

under	such	much	young	touch
use	your	you	unit	fuel
few	new	cute	human	music

1. chum ______________
2. outch ______________
3. sue ______________
4. uoy ______________
5. intu ______________
6. wef ______________
7. lufe ______________
8. redun ______________
9. chus ______________
10. hunam ______________
11. sicmu ______________
12. gnuoy ______________

Circle the misspelled words. Write them correctly on the lines.

1. Jim's dog ran undar the bed. ______________
2. Do you like her noo coat? ______________
3. What is yer name? ______________
4. That's a kute baby. ______________
5. Don't tuch the hot stove! ______________
6. Ann's sister is a yung lady. ______________
7. A fuo boys came to the party. ______________
8. Do you like rap moosic? ______________

Word Meaning

Draw a picture to show what each sentence means.

Kate found her kitten hiding under the bed.	Dad pumped fuel into the tank of his new car.
The young boy played music.	A few pennies were in the cute piggy bank.

My Spelling Dictation

Write the sentences. Circle the spelling words.

1. ______________________________

____

____

2. ______________________________

____

____

Word Study

Underline the words with the long **u** sound.
Circle the letters that make that sound.

use	such	few
young	music	under
your	you	unit
cute	much	new
fuel	human	touch

Write the spelling words that rhyme with these words.

1. crutch ______________
2. sung ______________
3. thunder ______________
4. shoes ______________
5. too ______________
6. flute ______________
7. few ______________
8. jewel ______________
9. Dutch ______________
10. store ______________

Fill in the blanks with rhyming word pairs from above.

1. Zeke hid ______________ the bed when he heard ______________.
2. They bought a ______________ pairs of ______________ shoes.
3. A ______________ little girl played music on her ______________.

Building Spelling Skills WEEK 6

Spelling List

This Week's Focus:
- Spell words that end with a silent e
- Spell homophones
- Compare past and present tense verbs

STEP 1 Read and Spell | **STEP 2 Copy and Spell** | **STEP 3 Cover and Spell**

fold

1. save
2. give
3. have
4. live
5. move
6. above
7. alive
8. alike
9. to
10. two
11. too
12. know
13. do
14. blew
15. blue
16. ______ bonus word
17. ______ bonus word

Visual Memory

Fill in the missing letters.

save	give	have	live	move
above	alike	alive	to	two
too	know	do	blew	blue

_____oo _____ike _____ew _____ow

_____ue _____wo _____o _____o

_____ove _____ove _____ave _____ave

_____ive _____ive _____ive

Circle the misspelled words.
Write them correctly on the lines.

1. There were tow plants in the pot. _____________
2. The girls looked ulike. _____________
3. His new bike is blew. _____________
4. Do you no what fish like to eat? _____________
5. May I hav a ride to school? _____________
6. Will you geve me some milk? _____________
7. Nat went too the zoo. _____________
8. Moov your bike out of the street. _____________

Word Meaning

Homophones are words that sound alike but have different spellings and meanings.

Choose the correct homophone for each sentence.

1. That little boy is ____________ years old.
   (to, two, too)
2. I want an ice-cream cone, ____________.
   (to, two, too)
3. Bring the plates ____________ the table.
   (to, two, too)
4. A strong wind ____________ the leaves off the trees.
   (blew, blue)
5. Did you see how ____________ the sky was today?
   (blew, blue)
6. When will you ____________ if you can go on the trip?
   (know, no)
7. There is ____________ more peanut butter in the jar.
   (know, no)

My Spelling Dictation

Write the sentences. Circle the spelling words.

1. ____

____

____

2. ____

____

____

Word Study

A present tense verb tells about what is happening **NOW**.
A past tense verb tells about what happened before.
Use the spelling list to find the present tense for each past tense verb.
Write the present tense words on the lines.

past tense	present tense	past tense	present tense
1. gave	______	5. did	______
2. moved	______	6. had	______
3. lived	______	7. saved	______
4. knew	______		

Fill in the correct verb form.

1. New people just ______ (move) in next door.
2. Do you ______ (know) how to make toast?
3. The man ______ (blow) up balloons and made animals out of them.
4. Have you ______ (save) the money you need for a new bike?

Draw lines to match these words to their opposites.

alive	different
alike	below
above	dead

Building Spelling Skills WEEK 7

Spelling List

This Week's Focus:

- Spell words with double consonants
- Divide words into syllables

Step 1 Read and Spell	Step 2 Copy and Spell	Step 3 Cover and Spell
1. missed		
2. willing		
3. balloon		
4. spelling		
5. pretty		
6. still		
7. off		
8. added		
9. letter		
10. different		
11. pattern		
12. middle		
13. Mississippi		
14. zipper		
15. carry		
16. ______ bonus word		
17. ______ bonus word		

fold

Visual Memory

Find the words hiding in this puzzle.

m	b	a	l	l	o	o	n	o	f	f	x	l
i	i	l	l	z	i	p	m	i	d	d	l	e
s	o	s	w	i	l	l	i	n	g	i	z	t
s	c	a	s	s	y	z	g	o	o	f	a	t
e	t	s	t	i	l	l	i	u	v	f	d	e
d	g	i	p	a	s	l	i	p	p	e	d	r
c	o	l	r	o	w	s	n	o	p	r	e	p
a	z	l	e	t	t	r	i	n	e	e	d	r
r	p	a	t	t	e	r	n	p	l	n	r	e
r	o	p	t	d	i	f	f	u	p	t	z	t
y	f	e	y	o	s	p	e	l	l	i	n	g

added
balloon
carry
different
letter
middle
missed
Mississippi
off
pattern
pretty
spelling
still
willing
zipper

Circle the correct spelling.

1. misst	missed	mised	missd
2. baloon	balon	ballon	balloon
3. pretty	pertty	preddy	prety
4. ledder	eter	leter	letter
5. differunt	different	diferent	diffrent
6. patturn	patern	pattern	pattren
7. carry	cerry	karry	kerry
8. ziper	zippir	zipper	zippre

Word Meaning

Fill in the missing words.

added	balloon	carry	different	pattern
middle	missed	off	Mississippi	letter
pretty	spelling	still	willing	zipper

1. Did you study for the _______________ test?
2. We sailed on the _______________ River.
3. I bought a shiny red _______________ for my little sister.
4. The _______________ on her jacket broke.
5. Will you help me _______________ this box into the house?
6. Who wrote you that _______________?
7. I went to a _______________ school last year.
8. Mother cut out the _______________ for a new dress she is making.

My Spelling Dictation

Write the sentences. Circle the spelling words.

1. ____

____

____

2. ____

____

Word Study

Divide these words into syllables.

Remember the rules:

- If a word has double consonants in the middle, divide between them.
- If a word has an ending, divide between the base word and the ending.

1. balloon bal loon
2. spelling spell ing
3. pretty ________
4. letter ________
5. added ________
6. pattern ________
7. zipper ________
8. willing ________
9. middle ________
10. carry ________
11. missing ________
12. Mississippi ________

Fill in the missing double consonants to make spelling words.

1. spe____ing
2. o____
3. sti____
4. mi____le
5. pa____ern
6. mi____ed
7. di____erent
8. Mi____i____i____i

Building Spelling Skills WEEK 8

Spelling List

This Week's Focus:
- Spell verbs that end with **-ing** or **-ed**
- Spell irregular past tense verbs

STEP 1 Read and Spell	STEP 2 Copy and Spell	STEP 3 Cover and Spell
1. swimming		
2. swam		
3. getting		
4. coming		
5. came		
6. having		
7. doing		
8. ended		
9. happened		
10. happening		
11. started		
12. joked		
13. received		
14. smiled		
15. smiling		
16. ______ bonus word		
17. ______ bonus word		

fold

Visual Memory

Circle the missing letters. Fill in the blanks.

1. swi_mm_ing m (mm)
2. ca______e m mm
3. ge______ing t tt
4. star______ed t tt
5. en______ed d dd
6. ha______ened p pp
7. smi______ed l ll
8. sti______ l ll
9. swa______ m mm
10. co______ing m mm
11. jo______ed k kk
12. recei______ed v vv

Write the correct spelling of these words.

1. swiming __________
2. geting __________
3. comeng __________
4. haveng __________
5. dooing __________
6. happend __________
7. happining __________
8. joket __________
9. smild __________
10. kame __________

Fill in the missing word. Use the correct ending.

1. Raul __________ (start) piano lessons last week.
2. Have you __________ (receive) your birthday present yet?
3. Why is she __________ (smile)?

Word Meaning

Fill in the correct form of the missing words.

1. We ____________________ in the river yesterday.
(swam, swimming)

2. They are going ____________________ today.
(swam, swimming)

3. What is ____________________ on that television program?
(happened, happening)

4. That is the same thing that ____________________ on the last show.
(happened, happening)

5. Who is ____________________ to the band concert?
(came, coming)

6. Many people ____________________ to hear us play last year.
(came, coming)

7. Karen ____________________ when she opened the front door.
(smiling, smiled)

8. Why was she ____________________?
(smiling, smiled)

My Spelling Dictation

Write the sentences. Circle the spelling words.

1. ____

____

____

2. ____

____

____

Word Study

Write the past tense of these words.
Use the spelling list.

1. joke	______________	5. end	______________
2. swim	______________	6. smile	______________
3. happen	______________	7. receive	______________
4. come	______________	8. start	______________

Add the ending **ing** to each base word.
What did you do to spell the word correctly?

	no change	double final consonant	drop **e**
1. swimming		✔	
2. get______			
3. receive______			
4. come______			
5. have______			
6. do______			
7. smile______			
8. end______			
9. happen______			
10. start______			
11. joke______			

Building **Spelling** Skills

WEEK 9

Spelling List

This Week's Focus:

- Spell words with long vowel sounds
- Add **-ed** to verbs

STEP 1 Read and Spell	STEP 2 Copy and Spell	STEP 3 Cover and Spell
1. way		
2. these		
3. niece		
4. might		
5. show		
6. float		
7. brain		
8. mean		
9. close		
10. tried		
11. cube		
12. uniform		
13. stayed		
14. price		
15. usually		
16. ______ bonus word		
17. ______ bonus word		

fold

ʼisual Memory

nscramble the words. Match them to the correct spelling.

1. yaw	close	8. beuc	price
2. thees	niece	9. ripce	float
3. neice	way	10. mitgh	cube
4. hows	these	11. foalt	uniform
5. anme	tried	12. niarb	brain
6. locse	mean	13. formuni	stayed
7. deirt	show	14. edstay	might

ircle the misspelled words.
ʼrite them correctly on the lines.

1. My new band youniform is silver. ______________
2. Cloze the door when you go out. ______________
3. The boys mite go fishing next Saturday. ______________
4. Put an ice kube in that glass. ______________
5. Grandpa staid in bed until 8 o'clock. ______________
6. The fox tryed to catch a rabbit. ______________
7. Can you shoo me how to play this game? ______________
8. Did you ever drink a root beer flote? ______________

Word Meaning

Complete the crossword puzzle.

Across

1. not kind
4. the cost
5. special clothing
8. to shut
9. this one and this one

Down

2. a girl relative
3. what you think with
6. the opposite of **sink**
7. a six-sided square
10. to remain

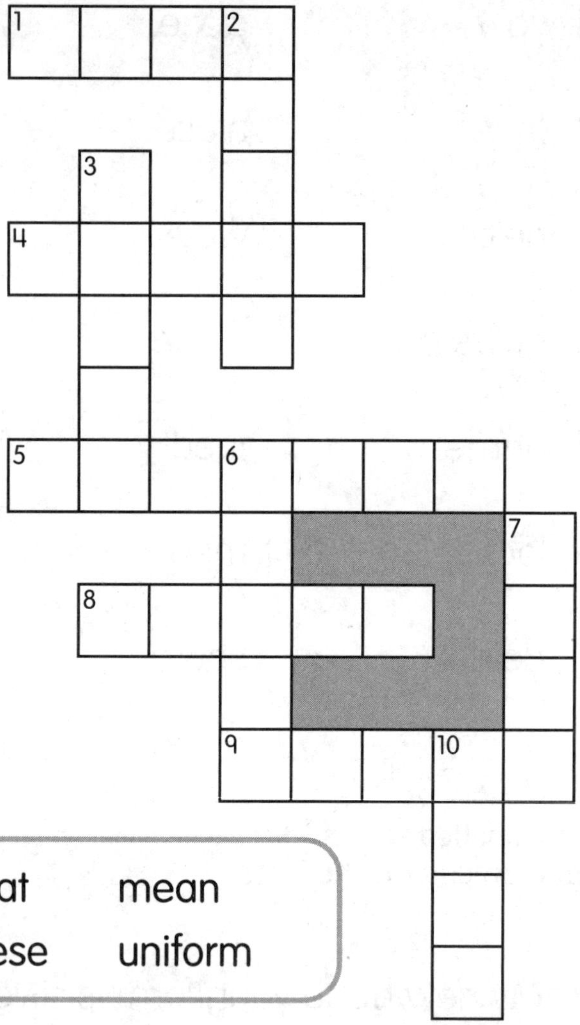

brain	close	cube	float	mean
niece	price	stay	these	uniform

My Spelling Dictation

Write the sentences. Circle the spelling words.

1. ______________________________

____

____

2. ______________________________

____

____

Word Study

Circle the letters that make the long vowel sound.
Write the long vowel sound you hear on the line.

1. way a	6. brain ____	11. uniform ____
2. these ____	7. mean ____	12. stayed ____
3. niece ____	8. close ____	13. price ____
4. show ____	9. tried ____	
5. float ____	10. cube ____	

Add **ed** to the words. Write the words in the correct column.

	no change	change **y** to **i**
1. stay	stayed	
2. try		
3. float		
4. show		
5. cry		
6. hurry		
7. plant		
8. worry		
9. play		
10. scurry		

Building Spelling Skills WEEK 10

Spelling List

This Week's Focus:

- Spell words with consonant digraphs **ch**, **sh**, **th**, and **wh**
- Identify the number of syllables in a word
- Recognize the /**sh**/ sound in **sure**

STEP 1 Read and Spell	STEP 2 Copy and Spell	STEP 3 Cover and Spell
1. children		
2. search		
3. teacher		
4. reached		
5. think		
6. together		
7. with		
8. where		
9. everywhere		
10. short		
11. push		
12. finish		
13. sure		
14. who		
15. whole		
16. ________ bonus word		
17. ________ bonus word		

fold

Visual Memory

Circle all the words that are spelled correctly.

reacht	finush	search
teatcher	whol	where
children	with	chilren
whith	shure	who
think	push	serch
everywere	sure	teacher
whole	poosh	thinck

Circle the misspelled words.
Write them correctly on the lines.

1. Hoo ate that hole cake?

    ________________ ________________

2. Can the childrun poosh the wagon?

    ________________ ________________

3. We can go when you finnish the shurt story.

    ________________ ________________

4. Where do you tink we should serch for it?

    ________________ ________________

5. Will you and your teecher go there togepher?

    ________________ ________________

Word Meaning

Answer the questions.

children	search	teacher	reached	think
together	with	where	short	push
everywhere	finish	sure	who	whole

1. Which ones are names for people?

   ________________ ________________

2. Which word means "all places"? ________________
3. What do you do when you use your brain? ________________
4. Which word means "to complete something"? ________________
5. Which word means "to look for something that is lost"? ________________
6. What is the opposite of...?

   part ________________ long ________________ apart ________________

My Spelling Dictation

Write the sentences. Circle the spelling words.

1. ____

2. ____

Word Study

Fill in the missing letters to make spelling words.
Write **ch**, **th**, **wh**, or **sh**.

1. ch ildren
2. sear______
3. ______ink
4. ______ole
5. ______ere
6. fini______
7. toge______er
8. pu______
9. tea______er
10. wi______
11. ______ort
12. ______o

Read the words.
Circle the number of syllables you hear.

1. together	1	2	3	4	9. sure	1	2	3	4
2. who	1	2	3	4	10. children	1	2	3	4
3. search	1	2	3	4	11. whole	1	2	3	4
4. teacher	1	2	3	4	12. finish	1	2	3	4
5. reached	1	2	3	4	13. push	1	2	3	4
6. think	1	2	3	4	14. where	1	2	3	4
7. with	1	2	3	4	15. short	1	2	3	4
8. everywhere	1	2	3	4					

Building Spelling Skills WEEK 11

Spelling List

This Week's Focus:
- Spell compound words
- Divide compound words into syllables

STEP 1 Read and Spell | STEP 2 Copy and Spell | STEP 3 Cover and Spell

fold

1. into
2. today
3. without
4. something
5. become
6. upon
7. myself
8. everybody
9. everyone
10. maybe
11. outside
12. basketball
13. homework
14. skateboard
15. earthquake
16. ______ bonus word
17. ______ bonus word

Visual Memory

Find the words hiding in this puzzle.

e	v	e	r	y	b	o	d	y	e	s	s
v	a	n	h	o	m	e	w	o	r	k	o
e	r	r	t	o	d	a	y	m	a	a	m
r	w	i	t	h	o	u	t	y	b	t	e
y	o	u	i	h	e	r	o	s	e	e	t
o	u	t	n	o	q	u	d	e	c	b	h
n	e	w	t	t	u	u	y	l	o	o	i
e	u	p	o	n	t	o	a	f	m	a	n
m	a	y	b	e	m	y	s	k	e	r	g
o	u	t	o	u	t	s	i	d	e	d	o
b	a	s	k	e	t	b	a	l	l	i	n

- become
- basketball
- earthquake
- everybody
- everyone
- homework
- into
- maybe
- myself
- outside
- skateboard
- something
- today
- upon
- without

Circle the 10 misspelled words.
Write them correctly on the lines.

Yesterday I finished my homewerk by misef. Then I went owtside and rode my skatbord to the park. Everbody was playing baskutball.

Evrywon was having fun when sumthing happened. The ground started to shake. It was an erthquak! When it stopped, we ran home wifout the basketball. Maybe it is still at the park.

________________ ________________

________________ ________________

________________ ________________

________________ ________________

________________ ________________

Word Meaning

Fill in the missing words.

become	basketball	upon	into	everyone
homework	skateboard	maybe	myself	outside
something	earthquake	today	without	everybody

1. Maurice received a ______________ for his birthday.
2. An ______________ made cracks in the walls of our house.
3. Our teacher said, "There is no ______________ ______________!"
4. ______________ strange ran ______________ the barn.
5. Once ______________ a time, there was a dragon that couldn't fly.
6. Do you want to ______________ a professional soccer player someday?
7. Can you wash the car ______________ any help?
8. ______________ is gone, so I am all by ______________.

My Spelling Dictation

Write the sentences. Circle the spelling words.

1. ____

____

____

2. ____

____

____

Word Study

Use the words in the word box to make compound words.

with	up	to	thing	quake
board	ball	day	every	body
come	side	my	may	home

1. basketball____________
2. be____________
3. earth____________
4. every____________
5. ____________one
6. ____________work
7. in____________
8. ____________self
9. ____________be
10. out____________
11. skate____________
12. some____________
13. to____________
14. ____________on
15. ____________out

Divide these words into syllables.

1. in|to
2. today
3. without
4. become
5. something
6. maybe
7. outside
8. homework
9. earthquake

Did you discover a new rule here about dividing words into syllables? Yes No

What is it? ____

Building Spelling Skills WEEK 12

Spelling List

This Week's Focus:

- Spell words with the vowel sound in **small**, **straw**, **song**, and **bought**
- Spell words with the short **u** sound spelled **ough**
- Add the endings **-er** and **-est**

STEP 1 Read and Spell	STEP 2 Copy and Spell	STEP 3 Cover and Spell
1. awful	____________	____________
2. called	____________	____________
3. falling	____________	____________
4. mall	____________	____________
5. small	____________	____________
6. straw	____________	____________
7. drawing	____________	____________
8. strongest	____________	____________
9. longer	____________	____________
10. song	____________	____________
11. along	____________	____________
12. bought	____________	____________
13. brought	____________	____________
14. rough	____________	____________
15. tough	____________	____________
16. ____________ bonus word	____________	____________
17. ____________ bonus word	____________	____________

fold

Visual Memory

Unscramble the words. Write them on the lines.

falling	awful	called	mall	straw
small	drawing	strongest	longer	tough
song	along	bought	brought	rough

1. awflu __________
2. decall __________
3. llam __________
4. gons __________
5. malls __________
6. olang __________
7. rouhg __________
8. lnoger __________
9. traws __________
10. darwing __________
11. srongtest __________
12. flaling __________

Circle the misspelled words. Write them correctly on the lines.

1. Adam made an ahful mistake.

   ____

2. Put the smal starw in the cold drink.

   __________ __________

3. He made a drawn of the stronust man in the world.

   __________ __________

4. Anna bawght it at the moll.

   __________ __________

5. Will you sing a longar sogn next time?

   __________ __________

Word Meaning

Answer the questions.

falling	awful	called	mall	straw
small	drawing	strongest	longer	tough
song	along	bought	brought	rough

1. Which word means "terrible"? __________
2. What could be used to make a bed for a farm animal? __________
3. What do you call a place with many shops all together? __________
4. Which word is a kind of picture? __________
5. What is the opposite of...?

   sold __________ shorter __________

   large __________ weakest __________
6. What does **straw** mean in this sentence? Circle your answer.

   I used a plastic straw to drink my milk.

   a. dried hay b. thin, hollow tube c. material for making popcorn

My Spelling Dictation

Write the sentences. Circle the spelling words.

1. __________

2. __________

Word Study

Underline the words with the sound of **a** in **all**.
Circle the letters that make the sound.

awful	called	tough
mall	song	along
rough	bought	straw
strongest	falling	brought
small	drawing	longer

Add **er** or **est** to make a comparison.

	er	est
1. strong	__________	__________
2. long	__________	__________
3. small	__________	__________
4. rough	__________	__________
5. tough	__________	__________

6. That wrestler is the __________ (strong) man I've ever seen.

7. Is a rabbit __________ (small) than a cat?

8. Mrs. Martin has the __________ (rough) bath towels I've ever felt.

9. Billy thinks he is the __________ (tough) kid on our block.

10. The yellow bus is __________ (long) than our truck.

Building WEEK 13 **Spelling** Skills

Spelling List

This Week's Focus:

- Spell words with the long **e** and long **i** sounds spelled **y**
- Spell the plural forms of words by adding **s**, **es**, or **ies**
- Spell the past tense of words by changing **y** to **i** and adding **ed**

STEP 1 Read and Spell	STEP 2 Copy and Spell	STEP 3 Cover and Spell
1. lady	______	______
2. ladies	______	______
3. surprise	______	______
4. surprises	______	______
5. toys	______	______
6. shoes	______	______
7. shy	______	______
8. cry	______	______
9. cried	______	______
10. study	______	______
11. studied	______	______
12. story	______	______
13. only	______	______
14. finally	______	______
15. family	______	______
16. ______ bonus word	______	______
17. ______ bonus word	______	______

fold

Visual Memory

Fill in the missing syllable to make spelling words.

1. la<u>dy</u>
2. ________ily
3. on________
4. ________prises
5. ________dies
6. stud________
7. fi________ly
8. ________y
9. ________ied
10. sur________

Circle the misspelled words.
Write them correctly on the lines.

1. The children gave Mother a big suprise. ____________
2. Put on your shoos before you go outside. ____________
3. The baby cryed for his bottle. ____________
4. Do you have a big famuly? ____________
5. Two ladys sang a song. ____________
6. Did you enjoy the storie? ____________
7. The game was finelly over. ____________
8. Have you studyed for the math test? ____________

Word Meaning

Fill in the missing words.

1. What ________________ was in that large box?
(surprise, surprises)

2. Both ________________ bought new hats.
(lady, ladies)

3. Did he ________________ clean his bedroom?
(finally, family)

4. She wants to ________________ the violin.
(study, studied)

5. My grandfather is full of funny ________________ that make me laugh.
(surprise, surprises)

6. I ________________ for a long time when my best friend moved away.
(cry, cried)

My Spelling Dictation

Write the sentences. Circle the spelling words.

1. ____

____

____

2. ____

____

____

Word Study

Write the words in the correct boxes.

cry	only	story	my	study	fly
lady	why	family	funny	shy	try

y says i	y says e
cry	

Write the plural forms. Mark how you changed each word.

		add s	drop e, add es	change y to i and add es
1. lady	ladies			✔
2. toy				
3. story				
4. shoe				
5. family				
6. rocket				
7. niece				

Building WEEK 14 Spelling Skills

Spelling List

This Week's Focus:

- Spell words with the vowel sounds in **push** and **do**

STEP 1 Read and Spell	STEP 2 Copy and Spell	STEP 3 Cover and Spell
1. looked	______	______
2. good	______	______
3. brook	______	______
4. football	______	______
5. cookie	______	______
6. stood	______	______
7. full	______	______
8. put	______	______
9. food	______	______
10. school	______	______
11. truth	______	______
12. room	______	______
13. true	______	______
14. chew	______	______
15. due	______	______
16. ______ bonus word	______	______
17. ______ bonus word	______	______

fold

Visual Memory

Find the words hiding in the puzzle.

f	g	t	r	u	t	h	c	h	f
l	o	o	k	e	d	r	o	c	u
f	o	o	d	o	o	k	o	o	l
t	d	p	t	c	h	e	w	o	l
r	u	u	u	b	r	o	o	k	m
u	e	s	p	t	a	t	h	i	h
e	s	c	h	o	o	l	x	e	e
n	o	s	t	o	o	d	l	m	w

brook	looked
chew	put
cookie	room
due	school
food	stood
football	true
full	truth
good	

Circle the misspelled words.
Write them correctly on the lines.

1. luked
2. good
3. brook
4. futbal
5. cookee
6. fud
7. full
8. poot
9. stood
10. schol
11. truth
12. doo
13. chu
14. true
15. ruum

Word Meaning

Complete the crossword puzzle.

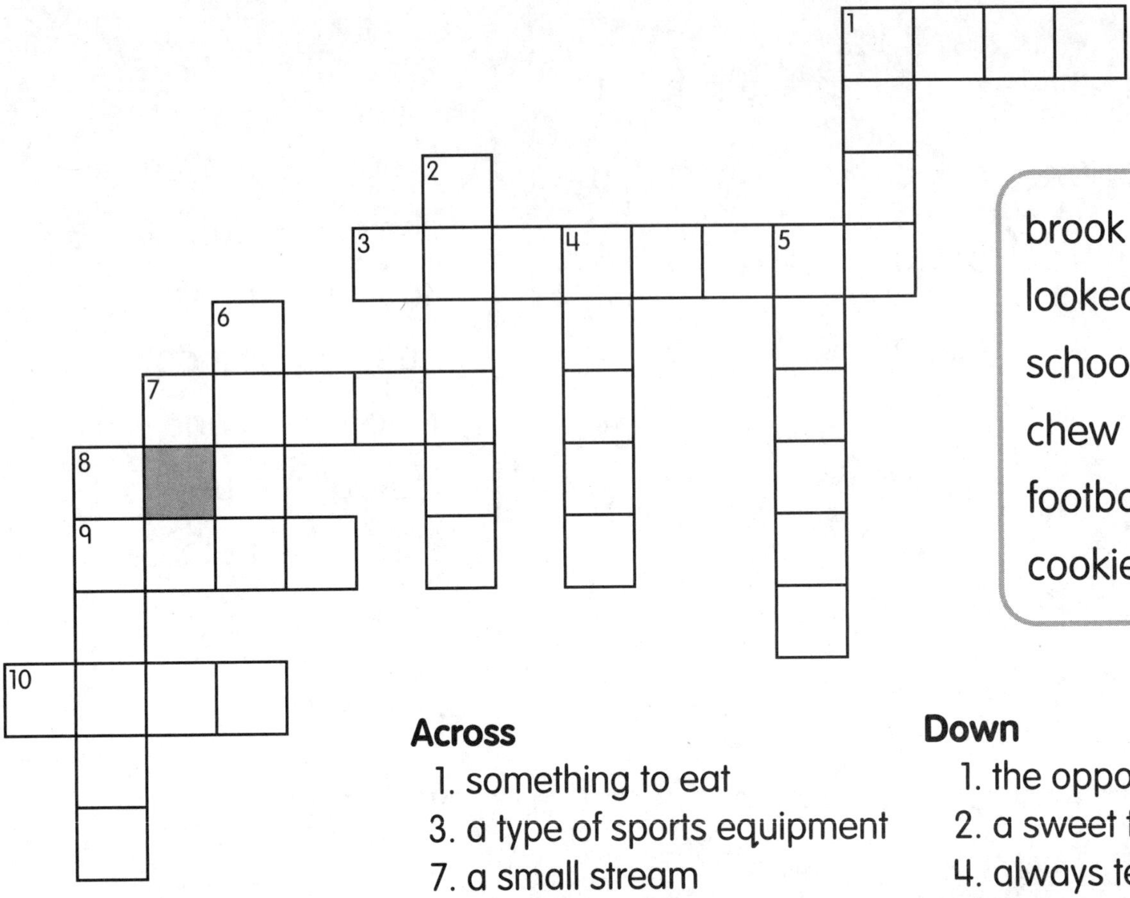

brook	food
looked	full
school	true
chew	truth
football	good
cookie	

Across

1. something to eat
3. a type of sports equipment
7. a small stream
9. to crush with your teeth
10. the opposite of **bad**

Down

1. the opposite of **empty**
2. a sweet treat
4. always tell the ____
5. used your eyes to see
6. not a lie
8. where you go to learn

My Spelling Dictation

Write the sentences. Circle the spelling words.

1. ______________________________

____

____

2. ______________________________

____

____

Word Study

Write the words in the correct boxes.

looked	good	truth	put	stood
food	brook	room	true	full
football	school	cookie	chew	due

sound of **u** in **push**	sound of **o** in **do**
looked	

Use the spelling list to find words that are the opposite.

1. empty ____________
2. awful ____________
3. sat ____________
4. remove ____________
5. lie ____________
6. false ____________

Building Spelling Skills WEEK 15

Spelling List

This Week's Focus:

- Spell words with **oy** and **oi**
- Spell words with the initial digraph **ch**
- Add the endings **-s**, **-es**, **-ed**, and **-ing**

STEP 1 Read and Spell	STEP 2 Copy and Spell	STEP 3 Cover and Spell
1. pointing		
2. oily		
3. boy		
4. voice		
5. oyster		
6. voyage		
7. loyal		
8. joined		
9. coin		
10. choice		
11. poison		
12. destroy		
13. enjoy		
14. choose		
15. chocolate		
16. ______ bonus word		
17. ______ bonus word		

fold

Visual Memory

Unscramble the words. Match them to the correct spelling.

1. yoil	voice	8. ocin	coin
2. cevoi	oily	9. ingpoint	joined
3. soyter	boy	10. cocholate	choice
4. joyen	voyage	11. edjoin	chocolate
5. yob	oyster	12. oichce	pointing
6. agevoy	loyal	13. sonpoi	destroy
7. loyla	enjoy	14. troydes	poison

Circle the misspelled words. Write them correctly on the lines.

1. My choyse is chocklate.

    ______________ ______________

2. Did you injoy your voyege?

    ______________ ______________

3. He will distroy the weeds without using poisen.

    ______________ ______________

4. The little doy is pointing at an oister.

    ______________ ______________

5. Which coyn did he chose?

    ______________ ______________

Word Meaning

Fill in the missing words.

1. We ate ______ (coins, oysters) on our sea ______ (poison, voyage).

2. ______ (Oyster, Chocolate) cake is always Paul's ______ (choose, choice).

3. Did that ______ (joined, boy) ______ (destroy, loyal) his toy truck?

4. Why are you ______ (pointing, oily) at that gold ______ (joined, coin)?

5. Don't use a loud ______ (choice, voice) while the baby is taking a nap.

6. Lock the box of insect ______ (chocolate, poison) in a cupboard.

My Spelling Dictation

Write the sentences. Circle the spelling words.

1. ______

______

______

2. ______

______

______

Word Study

Fill in the missing sounds. Write **oi** or **oy**.

1. b_____	4. _____ster	7. p_____son	10. c_____n
2. _____ly	5. v_____ce	8. p_____nting	11. enj_____
3. ch_____ce	6. l_____al	9. destr_____	12. j_____ned

Add endings to change the verbs.

	s or es	ed	ing
1. point	points		
2. join			
3. smile			
4. finish			

Add the correct endings to the verbs.

1. Norman was __________ (smile) at the funny television show.
2. The short hand on a clock always __________ (point) to the hour.
3. Betty always __________ (finish) her work before she plays.
4. Carlos is __________ (join) the Boy Scouts.

Building **Spelling** Skills

WEEK 16

Spelling List

This Week's Focus:

- Spell contractions
- Recognize homophones **it's** and **its**

Step 1 Read and Spell	Step 2 Copy and Spell	Step 3 Cover and Spell
1. don't		
2. didn't		
3. I'll		
4. I'm		
5. it's		
6. let's		
7. you're		
8. we're		
9. doesn't		
10. o'clock		
11. won't		
12. wouldn't		
13. its		
14. can't		
15. that's		
16. ____ bonus word		
17. ____ bonus word		

fold

Visual Memory

A contraction is a word formed from two words by leaving out some letters. An apostrophe is used to replace the letters.

Write the apostrophe in the correct place in these contractions.

1. don't
2. didnt
3. Ill
4. thats
5. its
6. cant
7. lets
8. youre
9. were
10. doesnt
11. oclock
12. wont
13. Im
14. wouldnt

Circle the misspelled words.
Write them correctly on the lines.

1. They din't like the scary movie. ________________
2. Did you know were moving when school is out? ________________
3. Why duzn't the clock work? ________________
4. Your going to Disneyland next week! ________________
5. Tat's Cindy's pet hamster. ________________
6. Its too hot to play outside today. ________________
7. Let's ask why they kan't come over. ________________
8. A'll bring my football to the game. ________________

Word Meaning

Write the contractions to complete the crossword puzzle. Don't forget to include the apostrophe.

Down

1. cannot
2. I will
3. does not
5. do not
6. of the clock
7. it is
8. we are

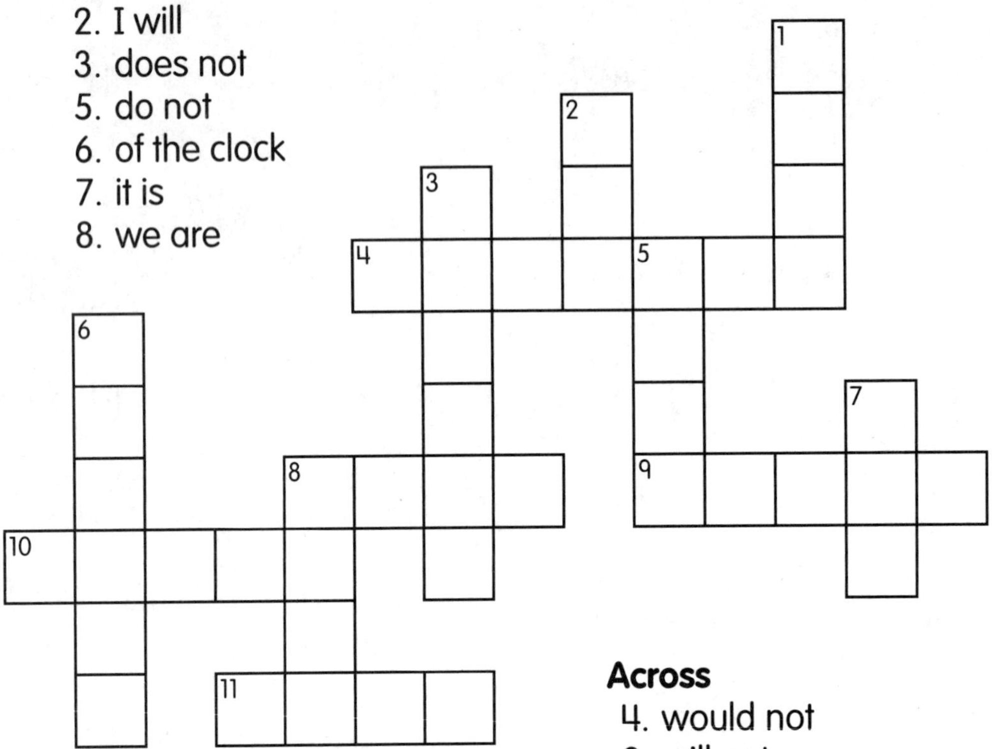

Across

4. would not
8. will not
9. that is
10. you are
11. let us

My Spelling Dictation

Write the sentences. Circle the spelling words.

1. ______________________________

____

____

2. ______________________________

____

____

Word Study

Answer the questions.

1. What is the long form of these words?

   won't ______________ don't ______________

2. Which spelling means "belonging to it"? its it's

3. Which spelling means "I will"? Ill I'll

What letter or letters are removed to make the contraction?

	contractions	missing letters
1. do not	don't	o
2. we are		
3. they are		
4. it is		
5. would not		
6. cannot		
7. I am		
8. that is		
9. does not		
10. did not		
11. I will		
12. let us		

Building Spelling Skills WEEK 17

Spelling List

This Week's Focus:

- Spell words with the vowel digraphs **ow** and **ou**

STEP 1 Read and Spell	STEP 2 Copy and Spell	STEP 3 Cover and Spell
1. follow	______	______
2. below	______	______
3. own	______	______
4. grown	______	______
5. town	______	______
6. ground	______	______
7. around	______	______
8. found	______	______
9. about	______	______
10. house	______	______
11. group	______	______
12. would	______	______
13. should	______	______
14. country	______	______
15. cousin	______	______
16. ______ bonus word	______	______
17. ______ bonus word	______	______

fold

Visual Memory

Fill in the missing letters. Write **ou** or **ow**.

1. t______n	6. c______sin	11. ar______nd
2. h______se	7. ab______t	12. gr______n
3. gr______p	8. ______n	13. c______ntry
4. f______nd	9. bel______	14. sh______ld
5. foll______	10. w______ld	15. gr______nd

Circle the 9 misspelled words in the paragraph.
Write them correctly on the lines.

My kussin went on a hike with a grup of children from toun. They fallowed a path bello a small hill. They walked arownd a grove of trees and saw a herd of cows resting on the groun. Then it was time for everyone to go to my cuzin's howse for lunch.

__________	__________	__________
__________	__________	__________
__________	__________	__________

Word Meaning

Fill in the missing words.

1. The prairie dog ______________ (below, town) is under the ______________ (country, ground).

2. My ______________ (cousin, group) lives in a ______________ (country, around) across the ocean.

3. A large ______________ (own, group) of visitors stayed at our ______________ (house, cousin).

4. The farmer's corn crop ______________ (around, should) be ______________ (own, grown) by now.

5. Kelly looked all ______________ (around, ground) trying to find her lost shoe.

6. Do you have your ______________ (town, own) computer at home?

My Spelling Dictation

Write the sentences. Circle the spelling words.

1. ______________________________

____

____

2. ______________________________

____

____

Word Study

Listen for the vowel sounds.
Write the words in the correct boxes.

grown	group	ground	about	below
town	follow	would	own	should
found	country	around	cousin	house

sound of **o** in **go**	sound of **ow** in **cow**	sound of **oo** in **too**	sound of **u** in **up**	sound of **u** in **put**

Use words from the spelling list to make rhyming words.

1. shout __________
2. mouse __________
3. dozen __________
4. soup __________
5. could __________ __________
6. show __________ __________
7. ground __________ __________
8. bone __________ __________

Building Spelling Skills WEEK 18

Spelling List

This Week's Focus:

- Review words with long vowel sounds
- Identify long vowels in open syllables

STEP 1 Read and Spell	STEP 2 Copy and Spell	STEP 3 Cover and Spell
1. April		
2. babies		
3. over		
4. hello		
5. even		
6. we		
7. silent		
8. tiny		
9. menu		
10. future		
11. dear		
12. raise		
13. white		
14. used		
15. those		
16. ______ bonus word		
17. ______ bonus word		

fold

Visual Memory

Match the parts to make words.
Write the words correctly on the lines.

1. A	ver	1. April
2. e	pril	2. ______
3. ba	ny	3. ______
4. si	u	4. ______
5. o	bies	5. ______
6. ti	ven	6. ______
7. men	lent	7. ______
8. fu	ture	8. ______

Circle the misspelled words.
Write the words correctly on the lines.

1. My grandmother says all babys are deer.

   ______ ______

2. Mr. Martin is going to raize tiney roses in his garden.

   ______ ______

3. It was sylent in the cave until someone yelled, "Heloo!"

   ______ ______

4. Last Aprul we painted our fence whyte.

   ______ ______

5. The teacher yousd thoze books in her class.

   ______ ______

Word Meaning

Answer the questions.

April	babies	over	hello	even
we	silent	tiny	menu	future
dear	raise	white	used	those

1. What do you use to choose a meal at a restaurant? ____________
2. Which word means...?

   time that hasn't happened yet ____________

   above something ____________

   not new ____________

   a greeting ____________

   no sound ____________
3. How do you change the word **baby** to make it mean "more than one baby"? ____________
4. What month comes after March? ____________

My Spelling Dictation

Write the sentences. Circle the spelling words.

1. ________________________________

2. ________________________________

Word Study

Read the words. Listen for a long vowel sound.
Write the words in the correct boxes.

April	raised	used	over	babies
tiny	menu	those	silent	hello
we	white	future	even	

long **a**	long **o**	long **e**	long **i**	long **u**

An open syllable has a vowel at the end. The vowel is usually long.

Divide these words into syllables.
Circle the open syllable or syllables in each word.

1. April (A) pril
2. babies ______ ______
3. over ______ ______
4. hello ______ ______
5. even ______ ______
6. lady ______ ______
7. silent ______ ______
8. tiny ______ ______
9. menu ______ ______
10. future ______ ______

Bonus: vacation ______ ______ ______

Building Spelling Skills WEEK 19

Spelling List

This Week's Focus:

- Spell words with the short **u** sound
- Spell words with the schwa sound
- Review words with long vowel sounds

STEP 1 Read and Spell	STEP 2 Copy and Spell	STEP 3 Cover and Spell
1. disagree		
2. again		
3. given		
4. other		
5. money		
6. problem		
7. does		
8. of		
9. some		
10. laid		
11. change		
12. tired		
13. read		
14. nice		
15. lower		
16. ______ bonus word		
17. ______ bonus word		

fold

Visual Memory

Find the words hiding in this puzzle.

a	g	a	i	n	c	h	a	n	g	e	p
l	a	i	d	p	r	o	n	i	o	x	r
o	o	s	v	o	u	t	t	c	c	f	o
w	m	o	n	e	y	h	r	e	a	d	b
e	e	m	g	q	n	e	b	y	n	o	l
r	h	e	e	t	i	r	e	d	t	e	e
a	g	d	i	s	a	g	r	e	e	s	m

again	nice
change	of
disagree	other
does	problem
given	read
laid	some
lower	tired
money	

Circle the 12 misspelled words.
Write them correctly on the lines.

Jack had a prblum yesterday. He wanted to red a good book, so he went to a nyce bookstore. Jack picke out a book and handed his muney to the clerk.

Jack said to the clerk, "This is not the write chanje."

The clerk counted the monny agin. Jack was rite. The clerk gave him some more mony, and Jack went home to reed his book.

______________ ______________ ______________

______________ ______________ ______________

______________ ______________ ______________

______________ ______________ ______________

Word Meaning

Fill in the missing words.

again	change	disagree	does	given
laid	lower	money	nice	of
other	problem	read	some	tired

1. ______________ Arthur have enough ______________ to buy a ticket?

2. Did the ______________ lady help you solve your ______________?

3. I ______________ with what I just ______________ in the newspaper.

4. My hen ______________ some ______________ her eggs in the weeds behind the chicken coop.

5. Harry was ______________ five dollars for cutting Mrs. Murphy's lawn.

6. Would you like to have ______________ of my chocolate bar?

My Spelling Dictation

Write the sentences. Circle the spelling words.

1. ____

____

____

2. ____

____

____

Word Study

Underline the words that have the schwa sound.
Circle the letters that make the sound.

about lesson

1. disagree	6. tired	11. problem
2. again	7. given	12. used
3. lower	8. nice	13. silent
4. laid	9. read	14. those
5. change	10. raise	15. tiny

Fill in the blank with a rhyming spelling word.

other	money	read	laid
change	nice	tired	some

1. arrange ______________
2. fired ______________
3. honey ______________
4. paid ______________
5. bread ______________
6. twice ______________
7. brother ______________
8. drum ______________

Building Spelling Skills WEEK 20

Spelling List

This Week's Focus:
- Spell words with the variant sounds of **g** and **c**

STEP 1 Read and Spell	STEP 2 Copy and Spell	STEP 3 Cover and Spell
1. city		
2. cereal		
3. face		
4. could		
5. guess		
6. huge		
7. age		
8. danger		
9. goose		
10. gone		
11. coast		
12. clean		
13. guard		
14. giant		
15. carton		
16. ________ bonus word		
17. ________ bonus word		

fold

Visual Memory

Find the words hiding in this puzzle.

c	e	r	e	a	l	a	g	e	d	o
g	i	g	u	a	r	d	o	m	a	c
u	o	t	c	a	r	t	o	n	n	o
e	x	n	y	c	e	r	s	h	g	u
s	s	e	e	f	a	c	e	u	e	l
s	a	n	g	i	a	n	t	g	r	d
c	o	a	s	t	q	c	l	e	a	n

age	face
carton	giant
cereal	gone
city	goose
clean	guard
coast	guess
could	huge
danger	

Circle the misspelled words.
Write them correctly on the lines.

1. age
2. cartun
3. sereal
4. citee
5. clean
6. koast
7. could
8. danjer
9. fase
10. giant
11. gawn
12. goose
13. gard
14. guess
15. huje

______________ ______________ ______________

______________ ______________ ______________

______________ ______________ ______________

Word Meaning

Fill in the missing words.

coast	city	age	guess
danger	clean	guard	giant

1. The movie star had a ____________ to protect her.
2. Have you ever been to New York ____________?
3. The warning sign read "____________! Falling rocks."
4. The magician could ____________ a person's ____________.
5. Did you help ____________ up the beach on Saturday?
6. Why does she always buy ____________-sized packages of everything?
7. I can see sailboats off the ____________.

My Spelling Dictation

Write the sentences. Circle the spelling words.

1. ______________________________

____

____

2. ______________________________

____

____

Word Study

The letters **c** and **g** make a hard and a soft sound.

Read each word and listen to the sound of the bolded letter.
Write it in the correct box.

a**g**e	**g**iant	**c**lean	**c**oast	fa**c**e
carton	**g**one	**g**uess	**c**ould	**g**oose
cereal	**c**ity	hu**g**e	dan**g**er	**g**uard

c		g	
hard /**k**/	soft /**s**/	hard /**g**/	soft /**j**/

Fill in the blanks with spelling words that mean the opposite.

1. country ____________
2. tiny ____________
3. safety ____________
4. dirty ____________

Fill in the missing spelling words and their opposites.

1. When faced with ____________, he ran for ____________.
2. The ____________ goat hid from the ____________ wolf.
3. He was ____________ in class this morning, but is ____________ now.

Building Spelling Skills WEEK 21

Spelling List

This Week's Focus:

- Spell r-controlled words with **or**, **er**, **ir**, **ur**, and **ear**

STEP 1 Read and Spell	STEP 2 Copy and Spell	STEP 3 Cover and Spell
1. word		
2. work		
3. world		
4. were		
5. first		
6. girl		
7. turned		
8. learn		
9. bird		
10. fire		
11. here		
12. nurse		
13. jury		
14. stirred		
15. wear		
16. ______ bonus word		
17. ______ bonus word		

fold

Visual Memory

Unscramble the words. Write them on the lines.

word	were	turned	fire	jury
work	first	learn	here	stirred
world	girl	bird	nurse	wear

1. rowk ____________
2. drow ____________
3. gril ____________
4. laern ____________
5. fier ____________
6. weer ____________
7. nuser ____________
8. brid ____________
9. rowld ____________
10. yurj ____________
11. frist ____________
12. raew ____________
13. ternud ____________
14. sterrid ____________
15. reeh ____________

Circle the 9 misspelled words.
Write them correctly on the lines.

Raul was on his way to wurk when he tirned a corner and saw a house on frie. Ferst, he called 911. Then, he looked around the house.

Raul herd a gril calling for help. He helped her crawl out a window.

At the hospital, a nurse took good care of the gerl. The child said, "I want to lurn how to be a nurs when I grow up."

____________ ____________ ____________

____________ ____________ ____________

____________ ____________ ____________

Word Meaning

Answer the questions.

word	work	world	were	first
girl	turned	learn	bird	fire
here	nurse	jury	stirred	wear

1. Who helps sick and injured people? ____________
2. Which spelling word means...?
   the earth ____________
   flames ____________
   mixed it up ____________
3. What do you call letters put together to represent something? ____________
4. Who decides if a person is innocent or guilty of a crime? ____________
5. Which spelling word is the opposite of ...?
   last ____________ boy ____________
   play ____________ there ____________

My Spelling Dictation

Write the sentences. Circle the spelling words.

1. ____________

____

____

2. ____________

____

____

Word Study

Building Spelling Skills WEEK 21

Circle the letters that make the /er/ sound in these words.

1. first 3. turned 5. word 7. faster
2. learn 4. girl 6. were 8. work

Fill in the missing letters to make spelling words. Write **er**, **ir**, **ur**, **ear**, or **or**.

1. n______se 3. w______e 5. l______n 7. w______d
2. b______d 4. w______ld 6. quick______ 8. st______red

Write the spelling word that rhymes with each of these words.

word	work	world	were	first
girl	learn	fire	wear	nurse

1. care __________ 4. burst __________ 7. bird __________
2. fur __________ 5. curl __________ 8. liar __________
3. clerk __________ 6. fern __________ 9. purse __________

Fill in the missing spelling words.

1. What are you going to ____________ to the party?
2. Where ____________ the boys going in such a hurry?
3. My dad has to ____________ in the garden this Saturday.
4. Her mother is a ____________ in Dr. Chan's office.

Building Spelling Skills WEEK 22

Spelling List

This Week's Focus:

- Spell r-controlled words with **ar**, **are**, **or**, and **ore**

STEP 1 Read and Spell	STEP 2 Copy and Spell	STEP 3 Cover and Spell
1. aren't		
2. partner		
3. hard		
4. chart		
5. farm		
6. start		
7. large		
8. more		
9. before		
10. horse		
11. north		
12. morning		
13. care		
14. stare		
15. warning		
16. ______ bonus word		
17. ______ bonus word		

fold

Visual Memory

Match the parts to make a spelling word.
Write the complete word on the line.

1. far	th	1. farm
2. lar	n't	2. ______
3. nor	m	3. ______
4. are	re	4. ______
5. sta	ge	5. ______
6. warn	fore	6. ______
7. be	ner	7. ______
8. part	ing	8. ______

Circle the misspelled words.
Write them correctly on the lines.

1. arent	6. narth	11. hourse
2. care	7. stayr	12. partnur
3. mor	8. morning	13. hard
4. charte	9. befor	14. warning
5. farm	10. start	15. larje

______ ______ ______

______ ______ ______

______ ______ ______

Word Meaning

Fill in the missing words.

1. His ______________ rode off ______________ daybreak.
   (partner, start) (horse, before)

2. Is it hard work to run a ______________ ______________?
   (care, large) (more, farm)

3. We must ______________ on our trip early in the ______________.
   (start, warning) (before, morning)

4. Read the ______________ on the ______________ before you dive in.
   (morning, warning) (start, chart)

5. It isn't polite to ______________ at people.
   (care, stare)

6. The explorer had a ______________ trip going by dog sled.
   (north, hard)

My Spelling Dictation

Write the sentences. Circle the spelling words.

1. ______________________________

____

____

2. ______________________________

____

____

Word Study

Fill in the missing letters to make a spelling word.
Write **ar**, **or**, **are**, or **ore**.

1. p__ar__tner
2. n______th
3. m______ning
4. c______
5. h______d
6. ______en't
7. bef______
8. w______ning
9. st______
10. l______ge
11. m______e
12. ch______t
13. st______t
14. h______se
15. f______m

Write the opposite of each word from your spelling list.

1. easy ______________
2. tiny ______________
3. less ______________
4. after ______________
5. south ______________
6. evening ______________
7. finish ______________

Fill in the missing spelling words and their opposites.

1. The ____________ giant and the ____________ elf were friends.
2. I take a walk in the ____________ and again in the ____________.
3. Migrating birds fly ____________ in the fall and ____________ in the spring.
4. I do my homework ____________ dinner, and then I play ____________ dinner.

Building Spelling Skills WEEK 23

Spelling List

This Week's Focus:

- Spell words with the vowel sounds in **to**, **top**, **wall**, and **up**
- Recognize homophones **threw** and **through**
- Spell words with suffixes **-less** and **-ful**

STEP 1 Read and Spell	STEP 2 Copy and Spell	STEP 3 Cover and Spell
1. threw	________	________
2. through	________	________
3. thoughtless	________	________
4. caught	________	________
5. fault	________	________
6. taught	________	________
7. because	________	________
8. one	________	________
9. once	________	________
10. water	________	________
11. watch	________	________
12. wanted	________	________
13. wonder	________	________
14. wonderful	________	________
15. walk	________	________
16. ________ bonus word	________	________
17. ________ bonus word	________	________

fold

Visual Memory

Find the words hiding in this puzzle.

w	a	n	t	e	d	e	d	b	e	c
t	h	o	u	g	h	t	l	e	s	s
h	r	t	a	u	g	h	t	c	w	o
r	e	w	a	t	e	r	o	a	o	n
e	w	a	a	n	d	o	o	u	n	c
w	f	a	u	l	t	u	n	s	d	e
w	a	t	c	h	k	g	w	e	e	t
o	n	c	a	u	g	h	t	x	r	e
n	w	o	n	d	e	r	f	u	l	d

because	through
caught	walk
fault	wanted
once	watch
one	water
taught	wonder
thoughtless	wonderful
threw	

Circle the misspelled words.
Write them correctly on the lines.

1. wundir
2. caught
3. walk
4. wunce
5. becuz
6. tawght
7. thoughtless
8. watur
9. through
10. fawlt
11. wanted
12. throo
13. wach
14. onederful
15. one

Word Meaning

Answer the questions.

threw	walk	one	through	wonderful
once	water	wonder	watch	thoughtless
caught	wanted	because	fault	taught

1. Which spelling words rhyme with ...?

   bought ________________ ________________

   new ________________ ________________

2. What does **watch** mean in this sentence? Circle your answer.

   You must watch your step when you climb a ladder.

   a. be careful b. something that tells time c. standing guard

3. Which word means "only one time"? ________________

4. What is the past tense of ...?

   catch ________________ teach ________________

   throw ________________ want ________________

My Spelling Dictation

Write the sentences. Circle the spelling words.

1. ____

____

____

2. ____

____

____

Word Study

Read the words. Listen for the vowel sounds.
Write each word in the correct box.

wanted	water	through	walk
threw	because	watch	taught
thought	caught	fault	

sound of **a** in **wall**	sound of **oo** in **too**

Add the correct suffix to the words.

-less means "without"

-ful means "filled with"

1. Morris had a ______________ surprise.
   (wonder)
2. It was ______________ of you to be late for the party.
   (thought)
3. The ______________ man helped fix the flat tire.
   (thought)
4. I always feel ______________ on my birthday.
   (joy)
5. A newborn kitten is ______________.
   (help)
6. Will you be ______________ and clean up that mess?
   (help)

Building Spelling Skills WEEK 24

Spelling List

This Week's Focus:

- Spell words that end with **or**, **ar**, and **er**
- Spell words with the final long **e** sound spelled **y**

STEP 1 Read and Spell	STEP 2 Copy and Spell	STEP 3 Cover and Spell
1. color	________	________
2. odor	________	________
3. farmer	________	________
4. calendar	________	________
5. dollar	________	________
6. party	________	________
7. liar	________	________
8. after	________	________
9. number	________	________
10. better	________	________
11. doctor	________	________
12. weather	________	________
13. every	________	________
14. forty	________	________
15. sugar	________	________
16. ________ bonus word	________	________
17. ________ bonus word	________	________

fold

Visual Memory

Match the parts. Write the words on the lines.

1. co	y	1. color
2. calen	ber	2. ______
3. part	lor	3. ______
4. ev	dar	4. ______
5. num	ery	5. ______
6. o	gar	6. ______
7. doc	dor	7. ______
8. for	tor	8. ______
9. su	ty	9. ______
10. weath	ter	10. ______
11. bet	er	11. ______

Circle the misspelled words. Write them correctly on the lines.

1. The calender cost one doller.

   ______ ______

2. Dad had a big partie when he turned fourty.

   ______ ______

3. You had bettir see the doctur about that bad cold.

   ______ ______

4. What nummer comes after nine?

   ______

5. Evry flower in the garden has a sweet oder.

   ______ ______

Word Meaning

Answer these questions.

color	odor	farmer	dollar	calendar
party	liar	after	number	better
doctor	weather	every	sugar	forty

1. Which letters make the /**er**/ sound in these words?

   liar __________ after __________ odor __________

2. What do you call someone who helps sick people? __________
3. What do you call someone who is not truthful? __________
4. Which spelling word has the /**sh**/ sound in **she**? __________
5. Which spelling word means “all”? __________
6. What is the opposite of...?

   before __________ worse __________

My Spelling Dictation

Write the sentences. Circle the spelling words.

1. ____________________

   ____

   ____

2. ____________________

   ____

   ____

Word Study

Underline all the words that have the /**er**/ sound in **her**.
Circle the letters that make the /**er**/ sound.

color	every	better
odor	calendar	sugar
party	watch	dollar
march	number	liar
weather	after	farmer

Divide the words into syllables.

1. color ____col or____
2. calendar ____________
3. better ____________
4. dollar ____________
5. farmer ____________
6. number ____________
7. party ____________
8. liar ____________
9. weather ____________
10. odor ____________
11. after ____________
12. sugar ____________

Building WEEK 25 **Spelling** Skills

Spelling List

This Week's Focus:

- Spell words with the /f/ sound spelled **ph**, **gh**, and **f**
- Spell words with the base word **happy**
- Spell words with the suffixes **-ly** and **-ness**

STEP 1 Read and Spell	STEP 2 Copy and Spell	STEP 3 Cover and Spell
1. phone		
2. photograph		
3. orphan		
4. alphabet		
5. graph		
6. nephew		
7. enough		
8. father		
9. half		
10. Friday		
11. cough		
12. unhappy		
13. happier		
14. happily		
15. happiness		
16. ______ bonus word		
17. ______ bonus word		

fold

Visual Memory

Match the parts to make a spelling word.
Write the complete word on the line.

1. Fri	phan		1. ______
2. fa	ew		2. ______
3. or	day		3. ______
4. neph	nough		4. ______
5. e	ther		5. ______
6. pho	hap	py	6. ______
7. al	to	bet	7. ______
8. un	pha	graph	8. ______

Circle the misspelled words.
Write them correctly on the lines.

1. fone	5. fotograph	9. orfan
2. haf	6. fadder	10. happiness
3. alfabet	7. nefew	11. enuf
4. cough	8. graph	12. Fritay

______ ______ ______

______ ______ ______

______ ______ ______

Word Meaning

Answer the questions.

phone	orphan	nephew	happiness	cough
alphabet	graph	enough	Friday	photograph
father	half	unhappy	happier	happily

1. What do you call a picture taken with a camera? ____________
2. What is the word for a child with no parents? ____________
3. What is a name for all the letters from **a** to **z**? ____________
4. Which spelling word means "all that is needed"? ____________
5. What do you do when you have a bad cold? ____________
6. Which spelling words are names for family members?

____________ ____________

My Spelling Dictation

Write the sentences. Circle the spelling words.

1. ____________

____

____

2. ____________

____

____

Word Study

Sometimes the digraph **ph** and **gh** stand for the /**f**/ sound.
Fill in the missing letters. Write **f**, **ph**, or **gh**.

1. ph one
2. enou____
3. or____an
4. ____ather
5. ____riday
6. ne____ew
7. hal____
8. gra____
9. al____abet
10. ____otogra____

Fill in the missing letters to complete the spelling word.

1. Grandmother has an old ph____________ of her mother.
2. The first-grade teacher wrote the ______ph________ on the chalkboard.
3. I ate __________f of the chicken on F____________.

A suffix is something you add to the end of words to change the meaning.
Change these words by adding a suffix.

ly means "in this way"

ness means "the state of being"

1. She climbed ______________ (slow) and ______________ (careful) up the ladder.
2. The explorers were surrounded by ______________ (dark) inside the cave.
3. Red Riding Hood skipped along ______________ (happy) to Grandma's house.
4. His ______________ (kind) filled my heart with ______________ (happy).

Building **Spelling** Skills WEEK 26

Spelling List

This Week's Focus:

- Spell words with silent letters
- Spell words with the prefixes **un-** and **re-**

STEP 1 Read and Spell	STEP 2 Copy and Spell	STEP 3 Cover and Spell
1. ghost		
2. neighbor		
3. high		
4. knew		
5. knot		
6. unknown		
7. rewrap		
8. wrong		
9. written		
10. wrapper		
11. unwrap		
12. climb		
13. limb		
14. gnaw		
15. gnat		
16. ______ bonus word		
17. ______ bonus word		

fold

Visual Memory

Find the words hiding in this puzzle.

g	h	o	s	t	k	n	e	w	z
n	e	i	g	h	b	o	r	r	w
k	x	g	g	i	r	l	e	i	r
n	w	n	n	h	k	i	w	t	a
o	r	o	a	a	g	m	r	t	p
t	o	t	t	s	w	b	a	e	p
u	n	k	n	o	w	n	p	n	e
o	g	u	m	c	l	i	m	b	r
i	n	u	n	w	r	a	p	g	o

climb	neighbor
ghost	rewrap
gnat	unknown
gnaw	unwrap
high	wrapper
knew	written
knot	wrong
limb	

Circle the misspelled words.
Write them correctly on the lines.

1. gost
2. naybor
3. hi
4. gnat
5. knot
6. knoo
7. unknone
8. rewrap
9. rong
10. written
11. onwrap
12. clim
13. limb
14. naw

_______________ _______________ _______________

_______________ _______________ _______________

_______________ _______________ _______________

15. The ribbon was tied in a not. _______________
16. Little nats flew around the fruit tree. _______________
17. A lim broke off the tree during the storm. _______________

Word Meaning

Complete the crossword puzzle.

Across

1. not known
4. to move up a ladder
6. to take off the covering
8. the spirit of someone dead seen by a person
9. a fastening made by tying string together

Down

2. a person who lives next door
3. the opposite of **right**
5. words were put on paper
7. a small insect
8. to chew on

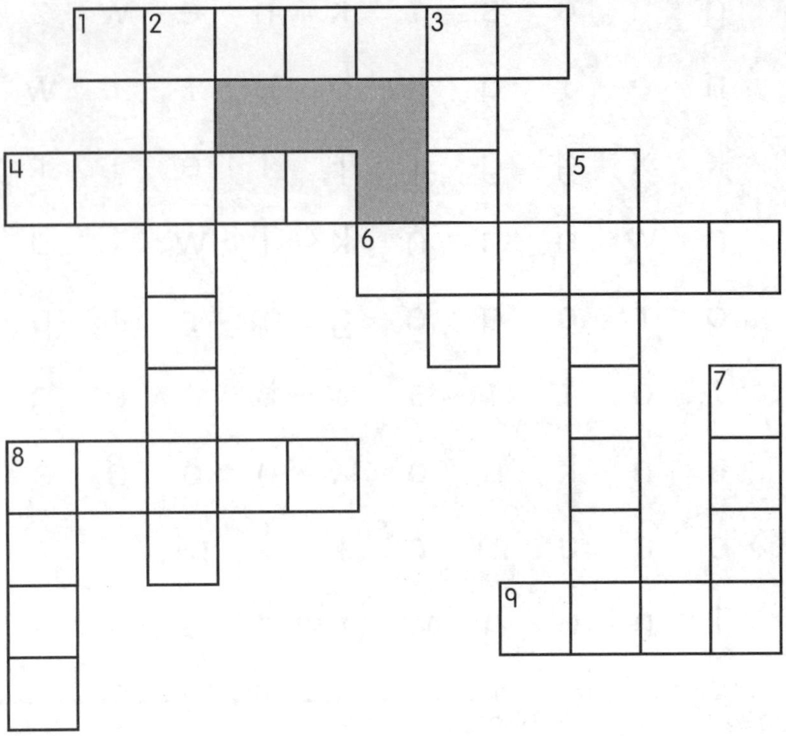

ghost	high	gnaw	limb	knot
written	knew	unknown	unwrap	wrong
rewrap	climb	gnat	neighbor	

My Spelling Dictation

Write the sentences. Circle the spelling words.

1. ______________________________

____

____

2. ______________________________

____

____

Word Study

Read each word.
Mark an X over the silent letters.

wrap knot

ghost	limb	knot	unwrap
high	knew	rewrap	climb
gnaw	write	wrong	gnat

Write the correct prefix in front of each word.

un means "not"
unhappy means "not happy"

re means "again"
reread means "read again"

1. My cat tore the paper on the gift, so Mother had to ______________ it.
(wrap)

2. The name of the artist was ______________.
(known)

3. People were ______________ of what to do after the earthquake.
(sure)

4. My homework paper was messy, so I had to ______________ it.
(write)

5. ______________ the present to see what is inside.
(Wrap)

6. Uncle Ted must ______________ the fence every five years.
(paint)

Building **Spelling** Skills WEEK 27

Spelling List

This Week's Focus:

- Spell words with the suffixes **-ful**, **-ly**, **-less**, **-er**, and **-est**

STEP 1 Read and Spell	STEP 2 Copy and Spell	STEP 3 Cover and Spell
1. useful	______	______
2. quietly	______	______
3. slowly	______	______
4. careful	______	______
5. careless	______	______
6. quickly	______	______
7. useless	______	______
8. worthless	______	______
9. fearful	______	______
10. fearless	______	______
11. joyful	______	______
12. smarter	______	______
13. fastest	______	______
14. funniest	______	______
15. happiest	______	______
16. ______ bonus word	______	______
17. ______ bonus word	______	______

fold

Visual Memory

Write the missing suffix to make a spelling word.

ful	ly	less	er

1. useful______
2. use______
3. quiet______
4. worth______
5. smart______
6. slow______
7. joy______
8. fast______
9. care______
10. care______
11. fear______
12. fear______

Circle the misspelled words.
Write them correctly on the lines.

1. Mother walked slooly and kwietly past the sleeping baby.

   ______ ______

2. Carla was joyfull when she won the ribbon for fastist runner in school.

   ______ ______

3. It is useles to do the job if you are kareless.

   ______ ______

4. Pete is the happyest person I know.

   ______

5. A feerless shepherd quikly chased away the hungry wolf.

   ______ ______

Word Meaning

Answer the questions.

useful	quietly	slowly	careful	quickly
careless	useless	fearful	joyful	worthless
smarter	fastest	fearless	funniest	happiest

1. What do these words do? **smarter** **fastest**

   a. name something b. compare something c. describe something

2. What do these words do? **thoughtless** **useful**

   a. name something b. compare something c. describe something

3. Which spelling word is the opposite of ...?

   quickly ____________ useful ____________

   careless ____________ saddest ____________

4. Which word means "afraid"? ____________

My Spelling Dictation

Write the sentences. Circle the spelling words.

1. ______________________________

____

____

2. ______________________________

____

____

Word Study

Add the suffix **est** to these words.
Mark what you did to change the word.

		no change	double final consonant	change **y** to **i**
1. fast	fastest	✔		
2. happy	________			
3. quick	________			
4. funny	________			
5. sad	________			
6. big	________			
7. smart	________			
8. silly	________			
9. small	________			

Add suffixes to the words to complete the sentences. Write **ful** or **less**.

1. Be care________ as you work so you don't make a care________ mistake.
2. The fear________ firefighter rescued the fear________ boy from the tree.
3. One sock is use________, but two socks are use________.

Building **Spelling** Skills

WEEK 28

Spelling List

This Week's Focus:

- Spell words with the long **a**, long **e**, and short **e** sounds
- Spell words in the **-other**, **-ead**, **-eat**, and **-ear** word families
- Recognize the /**ur**/ sound in **heard** and **early**

STEP 1 Read and Spell

STEP 2 Copy and Spell

STEP 3 Cover and Spell

fold

1. brother ____________ ____________
2. mother ____________ ____________
3. another ____________ ____________
4. field ____________ ____________
5. friend ____________ ____________
6. heard ____________ ____________
7. early ____________ ____________
8. friendly ____________ ____________
9. head ____________ ____________
10. near ____________ ____________
11. year ____________ ____________
12. shield ____________ ____________
13. eat ____________ ____________
14. measure ____________ ____________
15. break ____________ ____________
16. ____________ bonus word ____________ ____________
17. ____________ bonus word ____________ ____________

Visual Memory

Find the words hiding in this puzzle.

m	e	a	s	u	r	e	e	a	a
o	n	e	h	e	a	r	d	n	n
t	r	y	i	e	l	f	s	o	b
h	x	n	e	n	d	i	e	t	r
e	e	e	l	a	h	e	a	h	e
r	a	a	d	o	r	l	r	e	a
n	t	r	d	e	a	d	l	r	k
f	r	i	e	n	d	l	y	o	r
a	n	o	b	r	o	t	h	e	r

another	head
break	heard
brother	measure
early	mother
eat	near
field	shield
friendly	year

Circle the misspelled words. Write them correctly on the lines.

1. My muther and bruther have the same birthday.

   ______________ ______________

2. Trina hurd from an old frend today.

   ______________ ______________

3. We herd a noise in the empty feeld next door.

   ______________ ______________

4. Erly next yeer they are moving to Texas.

   ______________ ______________

5. May I eta unother slice of pie?

   ______________ ______________

Word Meaning

Complete the crossword puzzle.

Across

1. close by
3. the opposite of **sister**
7. a female parent
10. a piece of armor
12. listened to
13. a person who knows and likes another person

Down

2. the opposite of **late**
4. to chew and swallow food
5. to find the size of something
6. the top part of your body
8. to smash
9. an open area with few trees
11. January 1 to December 31

break	brother	friend	field	near
head	heard	measure	year	
shield	mother	eat	early	

My Spelling Dictation

Write the sentences. Circle the spelling words.

1. ______________________________

2. ______________________________

Word Study

Read the words. Listen for the vowel sounds.
Write the words in the correct boxes.

eat	friend	break	measure
head	field	shield	

long **e**	long **a**	short **e**

Change the beginning sounds to create new words.

____m__other	______ead	______eat	______ear
______other	______ead	______eat	______ear
______other	______ead	______eat	______ear
______other	______ead	______eat	______ear

Building Spelling Skills WEEK 29

Spelling List

This Week's Focus:

- Recognize homophones
- Review words with long vowel sounds

STEP 1 Read and Spell	STEP 2 Copy and Spell	STEP 3 Cover and Spell
1. they're		
2. there		
3. their		
4. soup		
5. night		
6. knight		
7. right		
8. write		
9. weight		
10. wait		
11. piece		
12. peace		
13. hour		
14. our		
15. wrote		
16. ______ bonus word		
17. ______ bonus word		

fold

Visual Memory

Match the scrambled word to the correct spelling.

1. ecape	their	7. twai	right
2. ousp	soup	8. peice	wait
3. threi	there	9. rou	piece
4. heret	peace	10. hrou	wrote
5. ightn	write	11. ritgh	hour
6. ritwe	night	12. rwote	our

Circle the misspelled words. Write them correctly on the lines.

1. Their going to get they're books.

   ____________ ____________

2. The brave night saved a princess last nite.

   ____________ ____________

3. Mom said to weight here for an howr.

   ____________ ____________

4. Hour friends came to dinner last nitgh.

   ____________ ____________

5. May I have a peace of there pizza?

   ____________ ____________

6. Can you right a recipe for that soop?

   ____________ ____________

Word Meaning

Fill in the missing words.

1. Can you put ____________ (their, there) coats in the closet over ____________ (they're, there)?

2. The ____________ (knight, night)'s fight lasted all ____________ (knight, night) long.

3. Try to ____________ (right, write) the spelling word ____________ (right, write) this time.

4. We spent an ____________ (our, hour) with ____________ (our, hour) grandfather.

5. What is the ____________ (wait, weight) of that huge hog?

6. That ____________ (peace, piece) of paper is a ____________ (peace, piece) treaty.

My Spelling Dictation

Write the sentences. Circle the spelling words.

1. ____

____

____

2. ____

____

____

Word Study

Read the words. Listen for the vowel sounds.
Write the words in the correct boxes.
Circle the letters that spell the sounds.

wait	peace	night	right	piece	stare
write	weight	beach	stair	sight	plane
flee	knight	plain	beech	flea	site

long **a**	long **i**	long **e**
wait		

Write the opposite of each word from the spelling list.

1. erase ________________
2. day ________________
3. here ________________
4. left ________________
5. war ________________
6. whole ________________

Fill in the missing words.

1. If you ____________ the word wrong, make it ____________.
2. The generals signed the ____________ treaty late one ____________.

Building Spelling Skills WEEK 30

Spelling List

This Week's Focus:
- Review long and short vowel sounds
- Review how to divide words into syllables

Step 1 Read and Spell	Step 2 Copy and Spell	Step 3 Cover and Spell
1. air		
2. against		
3. all right		
4. until		
5. presents		
6. beautiful		
7. favorite		
8. clothes		
9. people		
10. vacation		
11. remember		
12. already		
13. hospital		
14. minute		
15. straight		
16. ______ bonus word		
17. ______ bonus word		

fold

Visual Memory

Match the parts to make spelling words.
Write the complete words on the lines.

1. a	ents		1. ______
2. un	ute		2. ______
3. pres	gainst		3. ______
4. peo	til		4. ______
5. min	ple		5. ______
6. beau	ca	ber	6. ______
7. va	read	ful	7. ______
8. re	ti	tal	8. ______
9. al	pi	y	9. ______
10. hos	mem	tion	10. ______

Circle the misspelled words.
Write them correctly on the lines.

1. air	6. bootiful	11. already
2. alright	7. favrute	12. remimber
3. strate	8. clothes	13. hospital
4. against	9. peeple	14. minite
5. presunts	10. vacashun	15. until

______ ______ ______

______ ______ ______

______ ______ ______

Word Meaning

Complete the crossword puzzle.

Down

1. a place for the care of the sick or injured
2. not crooked
3. very pretty
5. men, women, and children
6. the one you like best

Across

4. gifts
7. a time of rest from school or work
8. what people wear
9. happened before this time
10. don't forget

already	clothes	people	remember	hospital
beautiful	favorite	presents	straight	vacation

My Spelling Dictation

Write the sentences. Circle the spelling words.

1. ______________________________

____

____

2. ______________________________

____

____

Word Study

Circle the letters in the words that make the given sound.

short u	until
short i	minute until
long i	all right
long o	clothes
long e	already remember
long a	favorite straight vacation

Divide the words into syllables.

1. against a gainst
2. presents ______
3. beautiful ______
4. favorite ______
5. people ______
6. vacation ______
7. minute ______
8. hospital ______
9. already ______
10. remember ______

My Spelling Tests

Using Your Spelling Test Forms:

First

Use the following pages for your Friday spelling tests. Write your answers on these forms.

Then

Record your score on your spelling record form on pages 156 and 157.

Spelling Test

Listen to the words.
Write each word on a line.

date

1.
2.
3.
4.
5.
6.
7.
8.
9.
10.
11.
12.
13.
14.
15.
16.
17.

Listen to the sentences.
Write them on the lines.

1.

2.

Spelling Test

Listen to the words.
Write each word on a line.

_______________ date

1. ______________
2. ______________
3. ______________
4. ______________
5. ______________
6. ______________
7. ______________
8. ______________
9. ______________
10. ______________
11. ______________
12. ______________
13. ______________
14. ______________
15. ______________
16. ______________
17. ______________

Listen to the sentences.
Write them on the lines.

1. ______________________________

____

____

2. ______________________________

____

____

Spelling Test

Listen to the words.
Write each word on a line.

_______________ date

1. ____________
2. ____________
3. ____________
4. ____________
5. ____________
6. ____________
7. ____________
8. ____________
9. ____________
10. ____________
11. ____________
12. ____________
13. ____________
14. ____________
15. ____________
16. ____________
17. ____________

Listen to the sentences.
Write them on the lines.

1. ____________

2. ____________

Spelling Test

Listen to the words.
Write each word on a line.

____
date

1. ______________________
2. ______________________
3. ______________________
4. ______________________
5. ______________________
6. ______________________
7. ______________________
8. ______________________
9. ______________________
10. ______________________
11. ______________________
12. ______________________
13. ______________________
14. ______________________
15. ______________________
16. ______________________
17. ______________________

Listen to the sentences.
Write them on the lines.

1. ____

____

____

2. ____

____

____

Spelling Test

Listen to the words.
Write each word on a line.

date

1.
2.
3.
4.
5.
6.
7.
8.
9.
10.
11.
12.
13.
14.
15.
16.
17.

Listen to the sentences.
Write them on the lines.

1.
2.

Spelling Test

Listen to the words.
Write each word on a line.

____
date

1. ________________
2. ________________
3. ________________
4. ________________
5. ________________
6. ________________
7. ________________
8. ________________
9. ________________
10. ________________
11. ________________
12. ________________
13. ________________
14. ________________
15. ________________
16. ________________
17. ________________

Listen to the sentences.
Write them on the lines.

1. ________________________________

____

____

2. ________________________________

____

____

Spelling Test

Listen to the words.
Write each word on a line.

____
date

1. ____________________
2. ____________________
3. ____________________
4. ____________________
5. ____________________
6. ____________________
7. ____________________
8. ____________________
9. ____________________
10. ____________________
11. ____________________
12. ____________________
13. ____________________
14. ____________________
15. ____________________
16. ____________________
17. ____________________

Listen to the sentences.
Write them on the lines.

1. ____

2. ____

Spelling Test

Listen to the words.
Write each word on a line.

_______________ date

1. _______________
2. _______________
3. _______________
4. _______________
5. _______________
6. _______________
7. _______________
8. _______________
9. _______________
10. _______________
11. _______________
12. _______________
13. _______________
14. _______________
15. _______________
16. _______________
17. _______________

Listen to the sentences.
Write them on the lines.

1. _______________

____

____

2. _______________

____

____

Spelling Test

Listen to the words.
Write each word on a line.

date

1.

2.

3.

4.

5.

6.

7.

8.

9.

10.

11.

12.

13.

14.

15.

16.

17.

Listen to the sentences.
Write them on the lines.

1.

2.

Spelling Test

Listen to the words.
Write each word on a line.

_______________ date

1. ____________
2. ____________
3. ____________
4. ____________
5. ____________
6. ____________
7. ____________
8. ____________
9. ____________
10. ____________
11. ____________
12. ____________
13. ____________
14. ____________
15. ____________
16. ____________
17. ____________

Listen to the sentences.
Write them on the lines.

1. ____________________________________

2. ____________________________________

Spelling Test

Listen to the words.
Write each word on a line.

____
date

1. ______________________
2. ______________________
3. ______________________
4. ______________________
5. ______________________
6. ______________________
7. ______________________
8. ______________________
9. ______________________
10. ______________________
11. ______________________
12. ______________________
13. ______________________
14. ______________________
15. ______________________
16. ______________________
17. ______________________

Listen to the sentences.
Write them on the lines.

1. ____

____

____

2. ____

____

____

Spelling Test

Listen to the words.
Write each word on a line.

______________________ date

1. ______________________
2. ______________________
3. ______________________
4. ______________________
5. ______________________
6. ______________________
7. ______________________
8. ______________________
9. ______________________
10. ______________________
11. ______________________
12. ______________________
13. ______________________
14. ______________________
15. ______________________
16. ______________________
17. ______________________

Listen to the sentences.
Write them on the lines.

1. ____

____

____

2. ____

____

____

Spelling Test

Listen to the words.
Write each word on a line.

____
date

1. ________________
2. ________________
3. ________________
4. ________________
5. ________________
6. ________________
7. ________________
8. ________________
9. ________________
10. ________________
11. ________________
12. ________________
13. ________________
14. ________________
15. ________________
16. ________________
17. ________________

Listen to the sentences.
Write them on the lines.

1. ________________________________

____

____

2. ________________________________

____

____

Spelling Test

Listen to the words.
Write each word on a line.

____
date

1. ____________________
2. ____________________
3. ____________________
4. ____________________
5. ____________________
6. ____________________
7. ____________________
8. ____________________
9. ____________________
10. ____________________
11. ____________________
12. ____________________
13. ____________________
14. ____________________
15. ____________________
16. ____________________
17. ____________________

Listen to the sentences.
Write them on the lines.

1. ____

2. ____

Spelling Test

Listen to the words.
Write each word on a line.

____
date

1. ________________
2. ________________
3. ________________
4. ________________
5. ________________
6. ________________
7. ________________
8. ________________
9. ________________
10. ________________
11. ________________
12. ________________
13. ________________
14. ________________
15. ________________
16. ________________
17. ________________

Listen to the sentences.
Write them on the lines.

1. ____

2. ____

Spelling Test

Listen to the words.
Write each word on a line.

____
date

1. ____________________
2. ____________________
3. ____________________
4. ____________________
5. ____________________
6. ____________________
7. ____________________
8. ____________________
9. ____________________
10. ____________________
11. ____________________
12. ____________________
13. ____________________
14. ____________________
15. ____________________
16. ____________________
17. ____________________

Listen to the sentences.
Write them on the lines.

1. ____

2. ____

Spelling Test

Listen to the words.
Write each word on a line.

______________ date

1. ______________
2. ______________
3. ______________
4. ______________
5. ______________
6. ______________
7. ______________
8. ______________
9. ______________
10. ______________
11. ______________
12. ______________
13. ______________
14. ______________
15. ______________
16. ______________
17. ______________

Listen to the sentences.
Write them on the lines.

1. ______________________________

____

____

2. ______________________________

____

____

Spelling Test

Listen to the words.
Write each word on a line.

____
date

1. ______________________
2. ______________________
3. ______________________
4. ______________________
5. ______________________
6. ______________________
7. ______________________
8. ______________________
9. ______________________
10. ______________________
11. ______________________
12. ______________________
13. ______________________
14. ______________________
15. ______________________
16. ______________________
17. ______________________

Listen to the sentences.
Write them on the lines.

1. ____

____

____

2. ____

____

____

Spelling Test

Listen to the words.
Write each word on a line.

_______________ date

1. ____________
2. ____________
3. ____________
4. ____________
5. ____________
6. ____________
7. ____________
8. ____________
9. ____________
10. ____________
11. ____________
12. ____________
13. ____________
14. ____________
15. ____________
16. ____________
17. ____________

Listen to the sentences.
Write them on the lines.

1. ____________

2. ____________

Spelling Test

Listen to the words.
Write each word on a line.

____
date

1. ______________________
2. ______________________
3. ______________________
4. ______________________
5. ______________________
6. ______________________
7. ______________________
8. ______________________
9. ______________________
10. ______________________
11. ______________________
12. ______________________
13. ______________________
14. ______________________
15. ______________________
16. ______________________
17. ______________________

Listen to the sentences.
Write them on the lines.

1. ____

____

____

2. ____

____

____

Spelling Test

Listen to the words.
Write each word on a line.

date

1.
2.
3.
4.
5.
6.
7.
8.
9.
10.
11.
12.
13.
14.
15.
16.
17.

Listen to the sentences.
Write them on the lines.

1.

2.

Spelling Test

Listen to the words.
Write each word on a line.

______________________ date

1. ____________
2. ____________
3. ____________
4. ____________
5. ____________
6. ____________
7. ____________
8. ____________
9. ____________
10. ____________
11. ____________
12. ____________
13. ____________
14. ____________
15. ____________
16. ____________
17. ____________

Listen to the sentences.
Write them on the lines.

1. ______________________________

____

____

2. ______________________________

____

____

Spelling Test

Listen to the words.
Write each word on a line.

____
date

1. ______________
2. ______________
3. ______________
4. ______________
5. ______________
6. ______________
7. ______________
8. ______________
9. ______________
10. ______________
11. ______________
12. ______________
13. ______________
14. ______________
15. ______________
16. ______________
17. ______________

Listen to the sentences.
Write them on the lines.

1. ______________

____

____

2. ______________

____

____

Spelling Test

Listen to the words.
Write each word on a line.

____
date

1. ____________
2. ____________
3. ____________
4. ____________
5. ____________
6. ____________
7. ____________
8. ____________
9. ____________
10. ____________
11. ____________
12. ____________
13. ____________
14. ____________
15. ____________
16. ____________
17. ____________

Listen to the sentences.
Write them on the lines.

1. ____________

2. ____________

Spelling Test

Listen to the words.
Write each word on a line.

____
date

1. ______________________
2. ______________________
3. ______________________
4. ______________________
5. ______________________
6. ______________________
7. ______________________
8. ______________________
9. ______________________
10. ______________________
11. ______________________
12. ______________________
13. ______________________
14. ______________________
15. ______________________
16. ______________________
17. ______________________

Listen to the sentences.
Write them on the lines.

1. ____

____

____

2. ____

____

____

Spelling Test

Listen to the words.
Write each word on a line.

____
date

1. ______________________
2. ______________________
3. ______________________
4. ______________________
5. ______________________
6. ______________________
7. ______________________
8. ______________________
9. ______________________
10. ______________________
11. ______________________
12. ______________________
13. ______________________
14. ______________________
15. ______________________
16. ______________________
17. ______________________

Listen to the sentences.
Write them on the lines.

1. ____

____

____

2. ____

____

____

Spelling Test

Listen to the words.
Write each word on a line.

____
date

1. ________________
2. ________________
3. ________________
4. ________________
5. ________________
6. ________________
7. ________________
8. ________________
9. ________________
10. ________________
11. ________________
12. ________________
13. ________________
14. ________________
15. ________________
16. ________________
17. ________________

Listen to the sentences.
Write them on the lines.

1. ____

2. ____

Spelling Test

Listen to the words.
Write each word on a line.

____
date

1. ______________________
2. ______________________
3. ______________________
4. ______________________
5. ______________________
6. ______________________
7. ______________________
8. ______________________
9. ______________________
10. ______________________
11. ______________________
12. ______________________
13. ______________________
14. ______________________
15. ______________________
16. ______________________
17. ______________________

Listen to the sentences.
Write them on the lines.

1. ____

____

____

2. ____

____

____

Spelling Test

Listen to the words.
Write each word on a line.

____
date

1. ______________________
2. ______________________
3. ______________________
4. ______________________
5. ______________________
6. ______________________
7. ______________________
8. ______________________
9. ______________________
10. ______________________
11. ______________________
12. ______________________
13. ______________________
14. ______________________
15. ______________________
16. ______________________
17. ______________________

Listen to the sentences.
Write them on the lines.

1. ____

____

____

2. ____

____

____

Spelling Test

Listen to the words.
Write each word on a line.

____
date

1. ______________________
2. ______________________
3. ______________________
4. ______________________
5. ______________________
6. ______________________
7. ______________________
8. ______________________
9. ______________________
10. ______________________
11. ______________________
12. ______________________
13. ______________________
14. ______________________
15. ______________________
16. ______________________
17. ______________________

Listen to the sentences.
Write them on the lines.

1. ____

____

____

2. ____

____

____

My Spelling Record

Week	Date	Number Correct	Words Missed
1			
2			
3			
4			
5			
6			
7			
8			
9			
10			
11			
12			
13			
14			
15			

My Spelling Record

Week	Date	Number Correct	Words Missed
16			
17			
18			
19			
20			
21			
22			
23			
24			
25			
26			
27			
28			
29			
30			

You are a SUPER SPELLER!

Name

Congratulations!!